End of the Line
The Moorgate Disaster

Richard M. Jones

LODGE
BOOKS

ISBN: 978-1-326-21141-7

Copyright © Richard Jones 2015

All rights reserved, including the right to reproduce this book, or portions thereof in any form. No part of this text may be reproduced, transmitted, downloaded, decompiled, reverse engineered or stored in any form or introduced into any information storage and retrieval system, in any form or by any means, whether electronic or mechanical without the express written permission of the author.

First published in Great Britain in 2015 by

Lodge Books
25 South Back Lane
Bridlington
www.lodgebooks.co.uk

This book is dedicated to the Emergency Services past and present.

Also by the same author

The Great Gale of 1871
Lockington - Crash at the Crossing
The Burton Agnes Disaster

Contents

Introduction	7
Foreword	9
1. Train 272	13
2. Into the Tunnel	26
3. Disaster	48
4. Trapped in the Darkness	52
5. Searching for the missing	87
6. Days of mourning, Days of grief	107
7. Questions and Answers	122
8. Causes and Conspiracies	132
9. Aftermath of a tragedy	149
10. Remembering	167
Afterword	189
Appendix A - Disasters and accidents on the London Underground	192
Appendix B - List of those killed in or as a result of the Moorgate crash	195
Acknowledgements	196
Further Reading	199

Introduction

The story of the Moorgate tube crash is one that has been surrounded by conspiracy and questions for forty years now. When I first heard of this disaster I was surprised to find that no memorial stood anywhere to commemorate what is today Britain's seventh worst rail crash. It seemed to me that people were more interested in blaming somebody than remembering the forty-three people who had been killed.

When I was first contacted about putting up a memorial I knew from the start that the stories needed to be told. I was amazed that so many survivors, firemen, police, ambulance crews and especially families had never had their voice heard. So many personal accounts of heartache and distress that normal, everyday people had to bottle up for decades. So many questions unanswered and nowhere to go to find the answers.

This book is dedicated to all those people; each and every one that got in touch with me to tell their side of the Moorgate story. I have sat through hours of interviews, spent weeks going around London through archives and libraries hunting for information. I have been told by those very people that my work has helped them come to terms with what happened. Reuniting survivors with their rescuers, answering questions whenever I have found the right information.

I have written this book to tell those forgotten stories. Starting in chronological order and giving insight into the real lives of the real people, many of them no longer here to talk about it. I have split the day of the disaster into two chapters over the same time period – one dealing mostly with the rescue operation, and another dealing with the families waiting at home and hospitals for news. For some it was the start of a never ending nightmare, for others it was the start of getting their life back and living it to the full.

Researching this terrible disaster has given me a wealth of knowledge and even made me a few friends along the way. The highlight of this project was the opening of a memorial in Finsbury Square after over thirty-eight years of silence. The victims of Moorgate will now always be remembered.

As I publish this book and move on to work on other forgotten disasters, I now turn this story over to the reader to look at my work and read the stories that have been untold for four decades. I hope I do the story the justice it deserves and finally put an end to the conspiracies that have reared their head over the years.

Anybody travelling in the vicinity of Moorgate station or Finsbury Square, I ask just one thing. Stop for a moment at the memorials and remember the people you are going to read about. You will never hear of more worthy heroes.

Richard Jones
January 2015

Foreword

Back in 1975 my name was Marian King, aged 20, and I was working in an office in Throgmorton Avenue. This was located just off London Wall and around the corner from Moorgate Underground Station. I had been working there for three years so I was familiar with the Tube journey from Highbury & Islington to Moorgate on the Northern City Branch Line which I made many times before and took for granted.

Friday 28th February 1975 started very much like any other work day, only I started out a little later than usual so was rushing to get to work on time. The train was already waiting and passengers boarding as I arrived on the platform. The first carriage was as usual very crowded, with more passengers trying to enter the first set of double doors. I decided to board the train using the second set of double doors of that carriage. This decision was one that later saved my life.

The Northern City Branch Line at that time started at Drayton Park and ran through the stations of Highbury & Islington, Essex Road, Old Street and terminated at Moorgate Station, shuttling passengers back and forth. At around 8.40am the train failed to stop at the Moorgate terminus and continued through the station and into the blind end tunnel on Platform 9. After having ploughed through the sand drag, it hit the end of the tunnel at around 30mph crushing the first three coaches into a space that would normally fit only one.

The first thing I remember following the impact was the firemen crawling through the wreckage calling to anyone who would answer them. I was trapped beneath a male passenger lying across my right leg causing it to be crushed. It took some time to move him as he had dislocated his shoulder and was in considerable pain. During this time I was given pain relief by the Doctors, freed from the wreckage and strapped to a stretcher. I was then turned sideways and passed along the narrow gap between the side of the train and tunnel. Throughout this ordeal the firemen remained encouraging and supportive. I was taken to the London Hospital, Whitechapel where for the next two weeks I was recovering from a torn ligament in my right leg, extensive bruising that covered my body making it very hard to move, and I had to regain my ability to walk. Most of my recovery was at home where I needed complete quietness to recover from the trauma, however the whole process of recovery took seven years. I still have numbness in my right foot and need to maintain the strength in my right knee joint with the help of my personal trainer. I am happily married to my husband Chris, who was my boyfriend at the time of the crash and has stood by me ever since. I also have two wonderful children, Leah and Stewart, both now grown up and making their own way in life.

At the time, 'The Moorgate Disaster', as it later became known, was a major media news item prompting discussions in Parliament and instigating various Inquiries. However, for forty years, there was not a plaque or memorial that marked this event. This was not until the families of the victims contacted Richard Jones, and in the short years of his involvement both a plaque and memorial have been erected. The plaque can be seen on the side of Moorgate Station and the memorial naming all those who died is on the green at Finsbury Pavement.

Both the plaque and memorial are not just to remind everyone of what happened that day but for me as a survivor an important tribute:

To remember all those who died by name, which is a very important part of the grieving process for all the families left behind.

A tribute to the Firemen, who battled against all odds to free all the passengers who were trapped in the wreckage.

A tribute to the Doctors and Nurses and medical staff, who administered painkilling drugs, operated to help free passengers, comforted and accompanied those on the long journey to recovery.

A tribute to the ambulance men and women who ensured all the injured were taken in a timely fashion to the various London hospitals.

A tribute to the Police who organised the crowds, cordoning off pathways and keeping exits clear and escorting the walking injured into awaiting ambulances.

And a tribute to all the Survivors who eventually 'walked away', some with life changing injuries. All who have a story about their journey of recovery and healing of both physical and mental injuries and who on the whole remain unknown.

It is all these stories that Richard Jones has tried to capture in this book; he has ensured that the memories of those involved are recorded and enabled them to have a voice after so long. This has allowed me the opportunity to meet fellow survivors, meet the families of those who died and above all to say THANK YOU to those who rescued and helped me, which the 'silence' of the past forty years did not address.

Marian Robertson
Survivor of the Moorgate crash
January 2015

1. Train 272

For anybody who has ever set foot in London they will always remember their first time. There is nothing like the feeling of the city's beating heart surrounded by the rush of the traffic. The city is awash with every kind of noise and feeling to stimulate your senses. You look around and see the famous black cabs, the businessmen, red phone boxes, buses, cyclists, aircraft, tourists, history and skyscrapers. Look further and you see the River Thames where a cruise will take you past the best of the best of the sights. Tower Bridge, Tower of London, *HMS Belfast*, the London Eye, the Shard, Houses of Parliament, to name but a few. Millions of people come to England's capital every year just to be a part of this amazing city. Thousands of years of history are there to see from the artefacts in the museums to the buildings that are still being used today. But the best thing about London is its people. Always there to show you how the "cockneys" do it, you will always be greeted with a warm smile and open arms no matter where you go. The people of London are proud of their city, the nation's capital.

London is a place where decisions are made that could affect the world, where the UK's financial market never sleeps and where you could visit every day for a year and still not see everything there is to see. But amazingly the biggest thing in London is hardly visible. Look around and you may see postcards of it, souvenir T-shirts and fridge magnets. Look further and you will see a small entrance to a set of stairs. Above these stairs is the famous sign that is known the world over, directing you to one of hundreds of passages to the most famous underground train network in history.

The London Underground started off in 1863 with the opening of what was known at the time as the Metropolitan Railway. Over time this network grew to become the most famous underground railway system in the world, although only 45% of it is actually underground. With 270 stations linking the various parts of the city, today the tube carries around a billion people per year. Workers, tourists, government officials and even royalty at times! This inspired underground railway networks around the world with major ones in Paris, New York, Tokyo and Rome, but it is London that has always remained the world's largest.

Right in the centre of London is the "City of London", a square mile of buildings, land and railway that has its own police force, councils, mayor and exclusive businesses. You always know when you have entered the City due to the statues of griffins that adorn the centre of the roadways and pedestrian walkways circling the City area. When you have passed those you know you have crossed the boundary, although most people walk past them every day without even noticing, many non-Londoners not even knowing they exist.

Now London itself has seen its fair share of tragedy in the last thousand years. Go back far enough and you see kings beheading queens, parliament beheading the king, terrorists plotting to blow up parliament. Everybody learns about the Great Fire of London in 1666 and the plague to affect the city the year before. But it has only been with the industrial revolution that London began seeing a different kind of disaster. Like everywhere else, whenever new types of transport came along it would take a major accident to make the creators realise that something needed to be made safer. The start of the factories and the creation of steamships led to progress, progress led to money and money led inevitably to building. The disasters that have befallen London in the last 150 years tell us that they can strike at any time and for apparently no reason. An investigation would have to be carried out to tell the world what went wrong and why. Who was to blame? What could we do to stop this occurring again?

Thankfully the major disasters are few and far between, but it was accidents like the sinking of the steamship Princess Alice in 1878 that led people to realise that so many people could die in such a short time and so close to the shore. That day, 640 people were lost in the collision between the *Bywell Castle* and the *Princess Alice*. This was to be repeated 111 years later at Southwark Bridge when the dredger *Bowbelle* ran into the pleasure boat *Marchioness* killing 51 people during a birthday party on board the pleasure boat. In 1952 a huge train crash at Harrow and Wealdstone killed 112 people, the worst rail crash in England, the second worst in the UK (only a troop train in Scotland was worse and that was when 227 died in 1915 after a collision at Quintinshill). These are only the big ones, there were hundreds of smaller accidents and disasters involving trains, ships, bombings, buses, war and smog to name but a few. Many of them are simply forgotten with the passage of time.

The thought of any disaster would send a chill up the spine of any member of the emergency services. But one man was not going to be unprepared when it did happen. Chief Inspector Brian "Bud" Fisher joined the City of London Police in 1951 and loved his job. He was second in command at Bishopsgate division and was involved in the filming of TV police drama *Softly Softly* which involved a tanker crashing into a school and the emergency services' response. It was a bit like The Bill was in the 1980s/1990s but this ran from 1966-1969, and it was this innocent TV entertainment that lit a spark in Bud Fisher's brain. What if there was another real-life disaster in London...but this time in the City of London area? A place this crowded, two different police forces (City of London and Metropolitan) nearby, fire brigades dotted all around either side of the Thames, hospitals crowded with rush hour traffic. It was going to happen one day, so why not plan for it now? He got to work on devising a major incident plan which took him on flights around Europe, talking to experts and police in Switzerland and Germany, gathering new ideas and learning how other countries' emergency procedures had worked well in times of crisis. He spoke to other forces in the UK and began consolidating what they already had and what was already in place. A huge plan was being devised for his division which, if successful, could be implemented further afield. This project took eighteen months to complete and he presented it to his division. Just a few months later he was tasked to do one for the three forces that made up the City of London division – Snow Hill, Bishopsgate and Wood Street. Already it had become a City of London plan instead of just a local Bishopsgate plan.

Brian's main success had been the development of a "Major Incident Vehicle", affectionately dubbed the "Mivvi Van". This vehicle had maps of the City and surrounds, all on wooden square blocks kept in sequence, so wherever the major incident occurred the site block could be placed in the centre of the board and the rest "jig-sawed" round it, so that the incident would always be in the centre of the map. Brian also studied other major incidents. At an air crash in Manchester he learned that the labels used there disintegrated in rain, had no string, and the pens used had ink which became illegible when damp. Brian's labels consequently were weather-resistant, stiff, had string, and chinagraph pencil stayed put. The Mivvi Van also carried miles of tape to secure areas, and plastic bags for bodies, property and exhibits...he had just about thought of everything! Even floodlighting, hitherto a problem, was solved by a telescopic high-power light which could be operated from within the vehicle.

Later on there was a competition, originated in the City Police, called the Neville Trophy. It was mainly to generate intensive training for the

Special Constabulary of the City, Metropolitan, Essex and Southend-on-Sea forces. There were VIPs involved such as the Chief Constables, HMI from the Home Office and the Special Constabulary Commandants: about 120 people plus four teams of six. The Inspecting Officer to judge turnout and drill was Mr Clisby of the London Fire Brigade. Brian Fisher's job was to organise a "Major Incident" in Guildhall Yard on which the teams' actions would be judged. Brian, as usual, did not "do things by half". On trailers, in quick succession, came a crashed helicopter, a telegraph pole, a fire engine and a British Petroleum tanker. The story was that the helicopter had crashed down, knocked over a telegraph pole which fell on the tanker, and the fire engine on call had run into the wreckage. This was one hell of a practical test! Said one officer, "Frankly the City should have been evacuated!"

Teams were given marks for first aid, finding the black box from the crashed aircraft and fire prevention. The watchers were exhausted just watching it play out, let alone the teams! After the tests the Guildhall Yard returned to normal, tea was taken and the winning team presented with the trophy.

The Mivvi Van was returning to the police garage at Wood Street when not long after, on 18 June 1972, an even bigger incident happened: a British Airways Trident aircraft had crashed in a field on take-off from Heathrow killing all 118 people on board. At the time it was Britain's worst air disaster (it is still second only to the 270 killed at Lockerbie in 1988). The City Police crew, with Brian Fisher still on board, went to help. The miles of tape were used to secure the area, all the kit within was fully tested and the Metropolitan Police were both pleased and grateful for this unexpected bonus and invaluable help. An amazing coincidence despite the tragedy of the loss of life. All went well with the disaster plan, however, a mishap occurred on the journey back to the City from London Heathrow; a member of the crew accidentally touched the operating mechanism of the telescopic light which promptly extended upwards, to be smashed to bits as they drove under the motorway bridge!

So with a plan and all the equipment ready and waiting, with a real life disaster attended and valuable training achieved (even though they couldn't save any of the occupants of the plane), the action plan was good to go. Without knowing it, Fisher had just become the hero in a story that would play out with tragic similarities to his plan.

*

The London Underground was the heart and soul of London, and working on the tube was one person who would never have a bad word to say about it. This was Leslie Benjamin Newson, a slim man of six foot one, and he was a tube train driver, or motorman as those in the trade call it, on the Northern Line. He had joined the company as a train guard and worked his way up in the last few years to taking his exams and becoming a motorman, working the District Line and spending the last fifteen weeks on the Drayton Park to Moorgate route. This was a very small stretch of the line, often called the Northern-City Line, which stopped at just a few stations before the journey back had to be taken. In around seven minutes the train would depart from either Finsbury Park or Drayton Park and call at Highbury & Islington, Essex Road and Old Street before ending the journey at Moorgate, a total journey of around 2 ½ miles. At that point the driver and guard would swap cabs and the train would do the entire journey again in reverse. Although a short line, this was a very important line as it took people into the heart of the City of London and during the rush hours it could become very cramped.

Newson was born in 1919 and was just twenty years old when he was thrust into the chaos of the Second World War. He had joined the army and was sent around the world doing his duty in the 8th Army. It was the outbreak of hostilities that led him to be at a Scottish training camp and there he met a woman from the small mining village of Harthill named Helen Wallace. She would be captivated by this brave soldier and what started out as a whirlwind wartime romance soon became apparent that it was more than just a fling. On 9th September 1941, at just eighteen years old, she became Mrs Helen Newson, much to the shock of her mother! They hadn't been married long when Helen fell pregnant and gave birth to baby George. Les was away at the time of the birth and didn't see him, but a tragic event meant that he never would when, not long after, baby George died of cot death.

Looking into the life of Les Newson it was obvious why Helen was so smitten by him. Described by his family as loving and generous, he would do anything to help anybody. He would always say "if you can't do somebody a favour with a good heart then don't do anything at all."

The end of the war in 1945 would see Les and many thousands of others have their military service come to an abrupt end. Les could now spend more time with his wife and decided to take Helen to see his family, but this happened just the once. He had lost his mother when he was just seven years old and his father had remarried since. With Les's siblings and now his stepmother's family on top of that, the amount of children in the family now ran into double figures. Unfortunately his stepmother treated her own children better than Les and his siblings. He did keep in touch though after he had left home, but when he introduced his new wife she was very rude to her and he left, never to return. "I have had that all my life, I am not carrying it on now," he said.

It was with great joy that Les and Helen would welcome their first daughter in December 1948 when Sandra was born. They were ecstatic, and in 1955 they were graced with a second daughter, Diane. By now Les was happy with family life and he kept himself busy on a daily basis by pursuing his hobbies. He loved to build his own furniture and was heavily into photography, even to the point of having his own dark room at his London home. When he wasn't taking photos he was repairing things or making new things for the house. His job with London Underground now became his life, he loved it and being ex-military it was obvious looking back that he was a big fan of travelling. He would take his motorbike and sidecar and all four of them would go on a road trip somewhere, kids crammed in the sidecar with Les and Helen on the bike, this being his main mode of transport for getting around. In the September of 1974 he flew over to Canada to see his brother for a few weeks and enjoyed it so much he was even talking of emigrating over there.

But it was the July of 1974 that stuck in Les's memory, and a day of pure joy when his daughter Sandra gave birth to his first grandson, Robert. Before he had even been washed and weighed Les had seen him and was over the moon. This was definitely a morale booster which he needed as the previous month he had been assaulted at work and this had left him shook up.

While Sandra had given him a grandson, Diane had given him a problem. Les had given her his old car, a blue Vauxhall Viva, as he knew she would look after it. That was before she had forgotten to check the oil level and caused the engine to seize up. The car was not worth the money to repair so it was a case of getting rid of it and finding a new one as soon as possible. She had £273 to spend on a new car, another Viva, but this time a white one. However, she wanted her dad to come with her to check it out before she handed over her hard-earned cash! Les took the money and put it in his work bag for safe keeping. It would be much easier for him to keep an eye on it when it was with him all day in his cab.

*

Friday 28th February 1975 was another quiet, cold morning when Les Newson got up for work at around 0400. He lived in a top floor flat out of the three floors and they had now lived here at 24 Palm Tree House on Barlborough Street, New Cross, for around ten years, renting it from Lewisham Council. Helen liked living in flats like this, it made her feel safe and if she was happy then Les was happy. Today he had a busy day planned, when he finished at around 2pm he was meeting Diane to help her buy the new car, and then he had to go back home to take down a set of huge curtains that Sandra had made and take them to the dry cleaners. He finished his usual two cups of tea and headed into the kitchen. He would always take his own milk and tea to work in his bag, so he filled his little glass bottle up with fresh milk and screwed the lid on tight before placing it in his work satchel. He also took extra lunch with him as he would normally have his first meal when he got to work as well as his normal lunch later on in his shift. As quiet as a mouse, Les closed the door behind him and made his way down the stairs, being careful not to bang too loudly and wake the neighbors. He opened the main front door and walked out into the cold, dark morning.

He caught the number 21 bus and changed once before arriving at Drayton Park Underground station. His first job when he arrived was to go over the train that he would be driving; a six-car train of 1938 stock, number 272, stood at the side of the platform. He had a number of checks to do before he could take on any passengers. He would open and close all doors, empty the air brakes, refill them and check all workings of the entire train's braking systems, usually with his guard. These checks had to take place every time you started a shift. Although he didn't say directly, he was concerned that some people were not checking the trains as thoroughly as they should. He was heard to say just two weeks before to his wife, "One of these days there is going to be an accident on this bloody line." But Les was a stickler for procedure, taking every daily task to military standards. He would always be twenty minutes early for work, enough time to have another cup of tea before his checks commenced. He would never turn up with a hangover, instead he would arrive smartly dressed, wearing his cap and tie, never removing either or unbuttoning his shirt, even when it became too hot in the summer. Each of his morning checks was done twice in accordance with the regulations. Although he could see a few of his colleagues skimping on standards he would never say a bad word about the company. As far as he was concerned the trains were safe and he would continue to be a loyal employee. John Baldwin, who had joined London Underground as a signal box boy in 1967 and was now a motorman himself, was the man who had been on that route before Les took over and always said that Les was a professional but quiet man.

That morning Les had a slight problem. Robert Harris, the guard, hadn't showed up for work yet. Until he made an appearance he would have to rely on one of the other guards to take his place for the first journeys. There had already been chaos nearby the previous day as a strike by signalmen over pay issues led to several major stations like Kings Cross and Liverpool Street being closed. Thankfully the turnout wasn't as disruptive as expected for the rest of the country as support wasn't that great and in some cases the disruption was barely noticed. That morning the news of the strikes was buried in the newspaper pages, the front page being reserved for the recent discovery in Hammersmith of an IRA bomb factory, found after a police officer was shot dead the day before that. In 1970s London there was always something making the headlines that would shock. Today was going to prove this beyond doubt.

*

It would be just before 0700 when 18-year-old Robert Harris would arrive at Moorgate station for his shift. He telephoned Drayton Park and spoke to Les Newson, telling him that he was there and would wait for him to make his return journey to pick him up. It was only a few minutes later that train 272 entered the station and the relief guard quickly handed over duty to Harris.

The train that Newson and Harris would be working today was the usual 1938 stock six-car tube train. A safe and reliable workhorse, which could carry up to 600 commuters, they had regular inspections daily, especially on the braking systems. The driver can open up the valve to charge the brakes with air and "release" the train, but if somebody was to open the valve while approaching the station it would send an audible alarm to the driver in his cab. Should the brakes "fail" then it would stop the train dead as any loss of air pressure would cause the brakes to close up – it was the pressure that was keeping the brakes prised apart in order for the train to operate. As he approached Moorgate station Les would cruise in very slowly – some say he was over cautious. He had a reputation for going slower than he should, in some cases he became a minute or two late on the turnaround, but he didn't care, as long as his passengers were safe that was all that mattered. He would be stood up as the cars came to a slow stop, with the guard preparing the rear end of the train to become the front on the return journey. Lights were changed from red to white and the reverse would happen at the front (which was now the rear) and the train would be ready within minutes to start the journey back up to Drayton Park all over again. If the guard was a guard-motorman then it wasn't uncommon for the two to simply stay put and swap jobs at every turnaround. That way they wouldn't have to keep walking up the platform and changing cabs on every journey. But Harris wasn't a motorman, at just eighteen years old he was just a guard so this didn't apply to him.

Dave Bolton had joined London Underground in 1952 at the age of fifteen. Starting off as a signal box boy he did his national service before shooting up the chain of Underground command, becoming area manager for the Drayton Park route in 1970. Dave had worked with Les Newson for a while, when he was in the Metropolitan Line depot and again at Barking when he was just a member of the station staff. Remembering him thirty-nine years later he would recall, "He was as always smartly dressed with his hat on, rolling a cigarette and looking across. A quiet guy, very good at his job, he was always on time."

Moorgate station itself was one of the first underground stations to be opened, in 1865, as part of the Metropolitan Railway, with ten platforms serving the Circle, Hammersmith and City, Metropolitan and Northern Lines. The Northern-City route started and finished on platforms 9 and 10, both of which were side by side separated by a partition wall and several exit routes to the main ticket hall. These platforms opened in 1904 and over a million train journeys have ended up on platform 9 by this point.

Leaving the station and heading back towards Drayton Park, train 272 in the journey departing from Moorgate would soon reach a crossover just yards into the tunnel where it would be sent back up the line, while the downward train would be heading down the opposite track. The tunnels themselves were larger than normal London Underground tunnels as they were initially built to accommodate main line trains as opposed to tube trains. At the ends of the lines were over-run tunnels, should any of the trains accidentally fail to stop in good time. On platform 10 there is an interesting historical site against the tunnel end wall. This is the Great Head Shield, used for expanding tunnels and digging. When the idea came to expand the line this was used to cut away at the earth, before it was decided that expanding was not a good idea and the shield was left there where it remains to this day. The 440ft long platform 9 however looks very different. The track runs on a downhill gradient of 1/150 into an over-run tunnel of 66 feet 9 inches long. In between the platform and the solid wall there is a sand drag designed to slow any runaways down leading out of the tunnel and several feet down the track. At the end of the sand drag, about halfway into the over-run tunnel, are the buffers. This should be more than enough to stop a train going at around 10-15mph that hasn't stopped on time. Many years ago a slow moving train had actually overshot one of the platforms and ploughed into the sand drag but thankfully no harm was done (This was reported in the Sunday Times on 2nd March 1975).

Very soon platforms 9 and 10 would be handed over to British Rail to use for mainline trains for which they were originally designed, so preparatory work was taking place on platform 10 leaving it closed to passengers. This was not a problem, because the line between Moorgate and Drayton Park was so short it was decided that platform 9 could handle the daily traffic on its own.

*

Drayton Park is one of the many London Underground stations that are in the open air. With a platform offering an upwards and downwards travel route, it could get very crowded during the early morning rush hours as many people living outside of the city changed at Drayton Park to get the connection to Moorgate. Les Newson had made countless journeys to and from this station just that morning; it was second nature to him and a very easy route, sometimes extending to Finsbury Park further up the line.

As train 272 stood idle at the platform ready to make its journey back south two unconnected men stood just feet away from each other. Bernard Marks and Fred Wonderling were both in the same age group heading to work in the City. As this was the start of the southbound journey they may have had to wait a few minutes longer for Newson and Harris to change around and get the train ready in all respects for departure.

Bernard was a 68-year-old who worked at Finlays tobacconist/newsagent at Liverpool Street. He would have normally got to the station ten minutes earlier than this but his car wouldn't start first time and that had delayed him. He had driven down to Finsbury Park and dropped his wife off before continuing on to Drayton Park station, leaving the car in the car park. As he had made his way onto the platform he saw an old friend whom he chatted to for a few minutes. He knew roughly where to stand on the platform to get a carriage where there would be a good seat on the train which in turn would give him a good place to depart when he reached his destination – nobody likes being in the middle of a crowd if you don't need to be! He got on carriage two and sat down, by now it was already getting full and his friend said that he would wait for the next train as it would be a bit less crowded. Sitting on a long row of seats facing each other, he settled down ready for the short journey into the City. Bernard lived locally and had had a bit of trouble with his son Laurence. Although it had been a week since he saw him, he strongly believed that he had every right to walk into his son's flat without even knocking and sit down. It was after all Bernard's flat that Laurence was paying him rent on, Bernard living with is own wife further down the road. He had had a confrontation with Laurence as he had already sat down in his son's chair after making a brew before he had even got out of bed. Bernard would argue that although Laurence was paying him rent it was still in his name so he would do what he wanted. "How would you feel if somebody just burst into your flat?" his son would say to him. He was furious his father felt that he had the right to just enter when he felt like it, as he never invited anybody into his home at the best of times. Bernard didn't like his son sticking up for himself so he had finished his tea and walked out. Thinking he had offended him too much in the argument, Laurence had said, "Well I hope this isn't going to be the last memory I have of him," wondering if he would return another day.

Sixty-year-old Frederick John Wonderling was also not close to his son. Also called Fred, he and his new step-mum hadn't got on with each other from the start, and although they were on speaking terms the seven year marriage had been a nightmare for Fred Jr. The Wonderling family was officially of German origin but the name was changed from Wunderling during the First World War due to the vast amount of anti-German feeling brought about by the sinking of the passenger liner *Lusitania* by a U-boat in 1915 which had killed 1198 people. Fred Snr. had been born the year before this incident just as the war was about to begin. When the Second World War broke out Fred was already in the army serving in the Royal Sussex Regiment, Glasgow Highlanders and even the Eighth Army in North Africa as the company Sergeant Major. He married 31-year-old sweetheart Violet in the July of 1940 and set up home in Shoreditch, London. When the war was over both Fred and Violet worked for Carrears, a tobacco company, and Fred even took a job on as a trolley bus driver. A very clever man, he had joined the army for a career and not just because of the war, teaching himself many useful skills along the way. Life was good and it got even better when they became parents to a daughter, who they named Margaret, in 1946 and later twins Fred Jr. and Brian were born in 1948. But tragedy was to hit the family in just a few short years when in 1964 his wife Violet died and seven years later his son Brian succumbed to polyneuritis. By 1967, however, he had married his current wife, May, and would be working only part time in the City due to his having angina. Fred Jr. never got on with May and by 1975 it had got to the point where Fred could only see his son in a pub so his son and his wife didn't have to meet. He went to meet his father with his 7-year-old son Johnny once, but sure enough May turned up much to the dismay of Fred Jr. A meeting like this wasn't something that he wanted; he wanted father and son time to talk about things and to rekindle the friendship they had always shared. Despite the differences with May, Fred Jr. would always say that he had a good father who was a great man. On the morning of 28th February 1975 Fred Snr. and May walked out of their flat and made their way to the station at Drayton Park which was only about 200 yards from their front door. She would see him off at the station and say goodbye to him like this every time. He made his way down the stairs and onto the platform, stepping into the carriage of train 272.

    Close by was 21-year-old student Javier Gonzalez, who was studying at the City of London Polytechnic where he had lectures later on in the morning just a short distance from Moorgate station. Getting up two hours earlier than usual, he had decided that he would travel early in order to get some studies done at the library, leaving his bedsit apartment and walking the short journey to Turnpike Lane Underground station, changing at Drayton Park and boarding the first carriage through the middle set of doors. He was familiar with the route the train would take and he would be right next to the exit when it arrived at the final destination. Finding an empty seat just by the doors next to a glass panel on his left side, he sat down facing the aisle and began to read his newspaper.

With the time at around 0837, guard Harris closed the train doors, with motorman Les Newson moving the train slowly forward. Gently picking up speed, Les drove his six-car train into the underground tunnel heading towards the next stop, Highbury & Islington.

2. Into the Tunnel

Just over a minute into the journey, train 272 pulled slowly into Highbury & Islington station, coasting slowly to a halt. As the doors opened a crowd of people boarded the train and squashed themselves into the carriages. One of these was 27-year-old Barry Coppock, who lived in Chingford with his mother, only a short bus ride away to his nearest station at Walthamstow Central. Normally he would use his season ticket to get through the barriers before heading towards the platform and boarding the train, getting on the Victoria Line and changing at Highbury. He worked just round the corner from the huge BP skyscraper near Moorgate station at Lloyds Motor Syndicate insurance firm down Finsbury Street. Today he had been unlucky and missed the train by seconds at Walthamstow and had to wait for the next one. Even unluckier for him the next one was cancelled, leaving him stood on the platform waiting for a third train. When it did arrive he boarded it for the short journey to Highbury where he would depart the train, change platforms and wait for the Northern-City Line southbound train to Moorgate. He would normally get into the front carriage, but as the doors opened it looked too crowded. He quickly headed further back into carriage four, ironically his only thought on this was, I don't want to be squashed up in the front carriage.

Barry wasn't the only person on that train who was working in insurance; in fact most people heading into the City had jobs that either involved some kind of insurance or stocktaking theme. One of these was Antony Byczkowski (pronounced *bish-koff-ski*) who was an insurance broker in the marine market at Lloyds of London. A slim and very shy 19-year-old man, he was very intelligent and had been all his life. A mathematical genius at school, he was so good at what he did he had Barclays Bank offer him a job immediately after leaving full time education, but he didn't want to go down that route. He was already employed by the insurance firm Lloyds while he was still at school and already they were talking of making him an executive of the business! Even at the tender age of four he loved playing around with numbers, even asking his mother Freda if he could start school early. Keeping his great intelligence to herself, Freda was forced to look shocked when the school told her of her son's incredible gift for mathematics. "All he wants to do is more sums!" the teacher said. "Really?" said his mother, laughing on the inside. Eventually he would run the teachers' tea and coffee float, going round collecting all the money owed from each class and working out the accounts for them. His father Zbigniew (pronounced *Spig-niff*) had been a Polish navigator in the RAF, who had come to the UK at the start of the Second World War, leaving his service behind when conflict ceased. Very few people would guess that Antony had any Polish connections other than his name, he always kept himself to himself, very few people knowing much about his personal life.

It was in 1949 that his parents had met, but Zbigniew had died at the age of 59 in the April of 1970 leaving Antony to be the man of the house at the age of thirteen, looking after three sisters and his mother. His youngest sister Annette would tell the author in 2014, "He was a bossy big brother, a very private man, but so good at maths. He would come into our bedrooms and fire maths questions at us to see how quick we could work it out." When he first started work he bought her a doll from a place in London, ironically it was one that was made in Poland, and she has treasured it ever since. He promised her one day that he would take her to see his favourite football team Tottenham Hotspur play. Now he was at the back end of his teenage years and no longer a child, he had a bit of an awkward relationship with his mother, calling her nosey whenever she asked him what he had been doing. A few curious incidents occurred in the short time before this: a pane of glass had suddenly fallen out of the window of his bedroom and landed in the room; and later a mirror broke injuring his wrists. All of these were simple accidents but there was a sudden increase in glass-related incidents for some reason! He did have a bad skin complexion which made it difficult for him to enjoy having his photo taken. One of his work friends was James Bowyer who remembers today the quiet young lad who worked hard for "probably no more than £750 a month". But at such a young age it was obvious that Tony would be going places in the coming years. Every morning Antony would leave the house early for work and this day was no different. Sometimes he would shout goodbye to his mother who would still be in bed, but today he didn't, probably believing she was asleep. He walked out of the family maisonette, where they had been living for around three years, and headed towards the station at Highbury & Islington.

Douglas Thomson was a 44-year-old government stockbroker and assistant internal auditor working for Mullens & Co at Moorgate. He had been working there a few years now, a long way from where he was from originally, Banff near Aberdeen. He was settled in London and lived on his own in Highbury New Park just a short walk from the station. As he was waiting for the train he saw a man he knew from old, 27-year-old stock jobber Jeffrey David Benton. Wearing an overcoat over his suit and a scarf round his neck, he turned to say hello and started chatting to him for a while.

Jeff was the eldest son of Thelma and Alan Benton and had been brought up in Tower Green with his younger brother Keith and two younger sisters Anne and Sarah. He had been educated at a school near Finsbury Park, leaving school at seventeen and going into the Stock Exchange as a career. His job was to do the deals for the company, known as a "jobber", (a jobber was somebody who would buy and sell shares through a middleman) and it was a good career to have, at one of the finest brokerage firms in the City at the time, Wedd Durlacher & Mordaunt. Although young, he was climbing the "City" ladder and his boss, Robert Wilson Stevens, praised him highly. At the age of twenty-three he married his 18-year-old fiancée Valerie in June 1972 after meeting at Hazelwood Lawn Tennis Club in Winchmore Hill on 31st October 1970. Life for Jeff and Valerie was going great, as she would recall in 2013: "We had decided to wait a while before starting a family as we were both young and wanted to establish ourselves. We bought a terrace house in East Barnet and our aim was to renovate this and build up some financial security before committing to family life. We bought a beautiful Irish Red Setter dog and 'Tessa' soon became part of the family."

Jeff enjoyed going on lads' holidays to Spain but at this moment in time his priority was decorating his new home in New Southgate with Val. He had seen his brother Keith over the Christmas period but because he was a teacher in the Midlands, time with him was pretty scarce. Douglas Thomson last saw Jeff a week or two before in a pub with his work friends, he was a little drunk and because he lived on the same route home he went with him on most of the journey to make sure he was OK. Jeff worked where Douglas used to work doing the same job so he knew what he was doing as a jobber. Today Jeff, like many other people in this story, was late. If he managed to get on in the first carriage then he would be able to run up the stairs and out into the street before the crowds of people took hold. Although the carriage at the front seemed packed, he got on and squeezed himself into a space.

Douglas joined him and then thought better of it, he got off and went down to carriage five which was slightly less crowded. He boarded with a work colleague of Jeff's, a man named Jim Payne, who was a messenger at his firm and also a friend of Douglas. Jim lived in Walthamstow and they had become good friends, even doing Doug's decorating at one point. Normally they would get off the train at Moorgate and grab a morning coffee together which is what they would probably do today. With the day ahead planned out, Douglas took his seat next to Jim on the right hand side of the carriage near the doors. He noticed a man sitting opposite and there were several empty seats; to say carriage one was packed there was plenty of room in here he thought, it's only about half full at best.

Peter Bradbury, a 23-year-old Yorkshireman, was born and grew up in Leeds before heading down to London in 1969 to attend Brunel University, studying maths with management applications. It was here he met his soon-to-be wife Janet King. Peter was very intelligent, he was the first lad from his school to attend university, receiving a 1st class honours degree, and he was working as an actuarial trainee at Equitable Life Insurance Co. in the City of London. He had been living with Janet at her parents' house in Edgware, North London up until recently when they had been closing a deal to buy their first house. In those few weeks they had to move out of her parents' home, as they had moved themselves further south, and look at temporarily renting a flat in the Highbury & Islington area while everything was finalised over a six-week period. It wouldn't be long now before they could finally set up a proper home together and get married. It seemed like the last year had been a testing time for him, as his father had died only a year or so earlier and being so far away meant that, with his family not having a phone in the house, he could only write to his mother, but he did this every day. She wouldn't be too lonely though as his two sisters were still in Leeds together. This February morning though, he was running a little late. He said goodbye to Janet and made his way to Highbury station, missing his usual train and instead boarding 272 which was now waiting to depart.

*

Just up the road from the station and down St Paul's Road was an off-licence run by the King family. Bob and Margaret would run the shop while their 19-year-old daughter Marian would head into the City every day to work at the Nat West bank head office on Throgmorton Avenue, dealing with unit trusts, stocks and shares. She had worked there since she was eighteen years old, doing work there during the week, while on a weekend her time would be taken up helping to teach children at the local St Joan of Arc Catholic School, spending her Saturdays with the pupils. With two different jobs taking up most of her days it was a wonder she found time for a love life, but she did, meeting the love of her life the year before, a man named Chris Robertson. They had met at a local youth club after being introduced by a friend of her brother and immediately hit it off. Very soon after Chris asked her out and they had remained in a relationship ever since. Every Friday it was "glam day" at work so Marian was encouraged to put lighter clothes on than usual due to the normal routine of having drinks in the afternoon. She had been running late today and had missed her usual 0830 train, but as she ran onto the platform train 272 was there and about to depart. She managed to get onto carriage one in the back half, holding onto the bobble hanging from the ceiling. With the last of the passengers now embarked, the doors slid shut and slowly departed. She was glad she was on it, she would have been annoyed if she had have had to wait for yet another one; luckily she had got on board and she was on her way at last. With her black handbag over her shoulder, she took out her book and started to read.

Dr Alistair Gordon was nine days away from his thirty-third birthday when he was heading into the City. Born in Hitchin, Hertfordshire, he went to Cambridge University where he gained a B.A. in Chemistry, going on to the University of East Anglia to gain his MSc in the September of 1965, and gaining his PhD in the October of 1967. He would later spend a year in Egypt at a university before being employed at a pig progeny research station near Letchworth. Now he had a job at British Petroleum in London, although he had still been living with his parents as it was cheaper for the time being. This had all changed just three weeks ago when he bought his own home in Islington and moved in, making him closer to work and quicker to get to the City.

*

Halfway through the journey into the City, train 272 coasted to a halt at Essex Road. Stood waiting on the platform amongst others was a 17-year-old lad called David Wilson. To begin that morning, like any other Friday, David had set off on foot carrying his workbooks for college; he had recently begun an engineering apprenticeship with a company in Islington and received time out to study engineering on a day release basis at West Ham College. He lived at the family home in Hume Court in Hawes Street, off Cross Street, Islington with his mum, Joyce. As always, he made for the furthest end of the platform, which therefore placed him in the front carriage of the train, in order to make a quick exit and change at Moorgate over to the District Line, travelling on to West Ham.

Stood next to David ready to enter carriage one was a young woman of twenty-one called Theresa Helen Hall, or Terry as she was better known. With long straight chestnut brown hair and beautiful blue eyes sporting long dark eyelashes, she was a very outgoing and funny girl, full of life and excitement. She worked at Peter Dumenil & Co Ltd in Smithfield: "Butchers to the catering company" they would announce on their headed letters. Terry had only worked there a few weeks but she got on with everybody and enjoyed it. Being a keen Arsenal supporter, she would go to their matches whenever she could and took a particular liking to one of the players, Charlie George (as well as the lead singer in Amen Corner – Andy Fairweather). She would go to a lot of the matches and one time her sisters Joy and Frances left school early in order for them to get tickets to one of the games for her and her other sister Lesley. Terry came from a big family: brothers Peter and Tony with her sisters Joy, Frances, Lesley and Christine together with her parents Joyce and John, living in a house in Upper Clacton, with Terry and Leslie sharing an attic room. One night she was accidentally locked out of the house and instead of waking the entire house up by hammering on the door, she climbed up the drainpipe and tapped on the window for Lesley to open it. Unfortunately Lesley was fast asleep and didn't wake up to the noise, so she shot back down the drainpipe and spent the night sheltered in the outside lavatory. Her sisters would remember her as "very mischievous – she once dropped a magazine on the track on the Underground and climbed down to get it!" The group of sisters used to love going down to the army barracks at Finsbury Square, managing to get mulberries from the soldiers stationed there so they could take them home for their mother to make into pies. When they weren't there, they were down at the local swimming pool nearly every night on Ironmonger Road in Finsbury. Terry was very particular about her hair, preferring it to be straight all the time. She wasn't too happy when she had to have it curled to be a bridesmaid at a wedding! Even her family said it looked strange seeing her with curly hair as it was just "not her look".

Trying to grow a fringe one time she got annoyed one day and started cutting at it, leaving a large bald patch on her forehead, much to the amusement of her sisters! A very creative girl, she would pick things up really quickly when she was being taught anything, learning how to knit and crochet. It looked strange when she did that as she was left-handed but she became really good at it over a short period of time. At family parties she would like to dance the night away and Joy remembers her today: "Every time I hear the song *Mony Mony* I think of Terry." Obviously a lasting impression of her! Terry would be the only person in the family who would use the Underground regularly, as there were no tube stations close to home and the rest of the family would use the local bus or get a taxi everywhere.

Her only weakness was the fact that she constantly felt sorry for people. If anybody had a tale of woe then they would get her attention and she would end up bringing them home for the family to meet. "She brought home all the strays...the only cat we ever had was what she had brought home," her sisters would say. When she was young she had measles which affected her eyesight drastically, this led to her having glasses, but she hated wearing them, preferring to just hold her books closer to her face, which she always did. In fact she never had her nose out of a book, despite her bad eyesight, and she was also never out of work, usually taking employment in offices, first at a hospital and now at the butchers. She was very hard working and in every job she was in she was well liked and popular. This week, however, she had been ill with a bad cold. After having several days off work she missed seeing her family on the Tuesday as normal and instead turned up on the Thursday. At this time of her life she was living between her family home and her boyfriend Rob's house on Essex Road. Her brother Peter's birthday had been on 9th February and she had returned back to the house to deliver a late present to him. She saw all of her family that day except her other brother Tony who was away at the time serving in the army. By now she had already had several days off work and felt like she was letting her boss down if she had any more time off. Besides, there was extra motivation to go to work today – it was payday! With that in mind she boarded the train, being no stranger to this line on the Underground as her beloved Arsenal stadium was right outside Drayton Park station. Now she had a choice of where to go: she could either get off at Moorgate and walk ten minutes down the road to work, or she could change trains and head to Farringdon station. She would worry about it when she got there, it all depended on the rushing crowds after all. It wasn't long before the train was back in the tunnel and thundering down the line to the next station.

As the train got into Old Street Marian King saw a woman get on and her hair was tied up really tight, not a piece out of place. "Oh god how did she get her hair that well?" she thought. (Tragically she would remember this image for all the wrong reasons as she would later see her dead beneath her.)

*

As train 272 headed back into the tunnel, a bunch of six carriages were now packed with people whose lives were about to change. Irishman Adrian Crotty was a 24-year-old working at Barclays Bank and had only been in London for around six months. He didn't like his job and was making plans to return to his native Kilkenny where his parents Rosaleen and Tom lived as well as his brother and sister. He was an extremely popular and outgoing man.

Geoff Marsh was another commuter in carriage one travelling into the city on his way to work. His school friend Patrick Roberts remembers him today. "My friend Geoff went to the same school as me, King Edward VI Grammar School in Chelmsford. He was a year older than me but I knew him well as we both shared a very long bus ride to and from school; one of the pitfalls of passing the eleven plus. His father was a vicar, minister or similar in a church (or chapel) in Abbess Roding, Essex and on occasion would rescue Geoff, myself and one other 'Grammar bug' when the buses failed – my first year at school was the famous 62/63 winter and smog was also very prevalent then. Geoff was pleasant and middle of the road, he did not shine out at school but then it was a bit of a hot house so that is no reflection and he was not bottom of the class. He and I vied for the same beauty from the mixed school down the road but there was no animosity as we were part of a queue! He also introduced me to pot in the 'summer of love and flower power' but again this is more innocent than it sounds – it was probably gravy browning!"

Margaret Liles had just celebrated her nineteenth birthday five days previously. She had double reason to celebrate now as that same day she had become a regular police officer at the City of London force after having been a cadet for the last eight months. As she was not attending training school until after Easter she decided that she would continue to commute from home and move into the section house after completion of all her training. This was working out pretty well as her journey into work was fairly easy. On 26th February she had been sworn in at Mansion House and as she left work the following day she was told not to rush in for Friday morning. Her mother had rung her up that morning and told her to hurry up or she would be late, but she reassured her that she had been told that it was OK to turn up late that morning anyway and not to worry. Starting her journey at Turnpike Lane she changed several times before she got in carriage one for the final stretch to Moorgate.

Stephen Payne had also wanted to be a police officer. He had joined the police cadet college two years previously to be part of the mounted divisions. Unfortunately he found that he had a heart murmur and his career was put on hold, and he was told that he wouldn't be able to return to any police training until he had turned eighteen. However, in 1970, he got a first class mark in a Theory of Music exam at the London College of Music. Perhaps his life was in music instead? A very thoughtful and caring young man, he would have been contemplating his choice of careers as he commuted from his home in Chingford via Highbury & Islington and into the City where he had his job at the Bank of America.

Not far from Stephen's house lived Janice Patricia Donovan, a 19-year-old secretary who worked in the City at a teaching firm for accountancy tutors named Foulkes Lynch. She was engaged to her boyfriend Roger but she still lived with her parents Joan and Fred in Billet Road, Walthamstow. She enjoyed flower arranging and playing the organ, kept herself to herself and was an ideal child according to her parents: "No problems whatsoever. She didn't drink, smoke or talk about anybody behind their back." They were exciting times for Janice and Roger, they had just had their mortgage application approved days before and the house in Chelmsford they wanted was back on the market after the buyer had suddenly died, leaving the young couple able to snap it up while they could. Tonight she would entertain her parents and show them the new house after they had all come home from work. Wearing a blue coat over a red jumper, she said goodbye to her parents and headed down the road. She met the woman who lived next door as she went to the post box and stood chatting to her for a few minutes before heading to the bus stop to take the short journey to the Underground station at Blackhorse Road, changing at Highbury for the City.

Also getting on the train at Blackhorse Road was 23-year-old Eileen Smith who would take the same route via the Victoria Line to Highbury where she would arrive at Moorgate close to where she worked in Gresham Street. As she got to Highbury, she noticed that the train was already there and ready to leave, so she ran to catch it and only just made it, entering carriage one. This was good because it could mean she would turn up early for work! The train was pretty full and there were no seats left, but not to worry, she would just stand as it was not far to go.

*

Banking was a significant industry for the City with thousands of people heading to various banks to start a career in the financial sector, some coming into such jobs straight from school. One of these was 17-year-old Janet Cook, who had secured a job at Nat West as a bank counter clerk. A very quiet girl, she had only really recently come out of her shell and had started to enjoy herself, even taking a trip to Spain with her cousin a few months back. She loved going out with the lads she knew, and one time when she went shopping with her mother she came back and said sarcastically, "I'm not going with her again…she turns the shop over!" Having had trouble with her eyesight from a young age, she wore contact lenses after having her eyes checked out for them at fourteen.

Right at the front of carriage one was 59-year-old Thomas Henry Thrower. A portly man of around 5ft 11ins tall, he had recently given up smoking after problems with his lungs. As he was now no longer a smoker he would be in the first carriage instead of the back. Thomas had lived a good life and always loved a bit of gambling – cards, dogs, horses, you name it – and he really enjoyed the horse racing on a colour TV! He was really into his boxing and even managed the Wingate Amateur Boxing Club, a Jewish club named after General Wingate, although he was the only non-Jew there at the time. If there was ever a big boxing match being fought he would dress up to impress and get involved in showing people to seats and making sure those in the audience were having a good time. He was a lover of hard work and always believed in it, this is most likely from his father Frederick who would be described as a hard taskmaster by those who knew him. Having three brothers, Thomas had lost his mother when he was a small child while she was giving birth, on top of that he also suffered the grief of losing his two sisters when they were very young, so it was up to Frederick to bring up the four lads all by himself in 1920's London. The death of his mother hit Thomas hard, especially in the initial stages when he first learned of her passing. An uncle simply came up to him and said, "Go tell your dad that your mum's just died." For a 12-year-old boy that would have hit him hard; he would later write a poem about his mother and pass it down to his own son years after.

A few years before the outbreak of the Second World War, Thomas joined the Territorial Army in the Sherwood Foresters Regiment, mostly taking him around the UK instead of heading off abroad. But this all changed when war broke out in 1939 and he got the chance to join the military police. With him and his men getting ready to start their training for duty in North Africa, he suddenly contracted pneumonia and had to stay behind in Britain to recover. He felt really bad about this as they had all been shipped out leaving him alone. At this point the decided to apply to be part of the air crew in the RAF so he could be part of the bomber crews. This was not to be, due to him having a family by now and they would only take on single men, so he stayed with the military police right up to the end of the war when he was demobbed.

The war had a huge impact on the Thrower family in more ways than one. Thomas had met a woman named Frances Swan and had married her in 1940, living close by in the Islington area, they would eventually move in with Frances's family. During a bombing raid in the infamous blitz on London, a bomb landed close by and failed to explode, leading to them all having to evacuate the area while it was diffused. When further raids occurred on London in the coming nights their home took a direct hit while they were out visiting family. The neighbours were all killed instantly and the mounds of rubble were testament to taking heed of the A.R.P. wardens' warnings to get away and take shelter. However, when the rubble was being cleared one of Frances's sisters kept saying that she was hearing voices. This was dismissed as nothing as she had a reputation for talking nonsense, but she persisted and kept telling them that there was a definite voice coming from the piles of rubble. Sure enough the persistence paid off and three survivors were found and taken out of the remains of the house. This remarkable rescue made local newspaper headlines the following day.

It was in 1943 that Thomas and Frances had a son whom they named Kenneth, but before long Thomas was back to work fighting for his country, doing so for the next two years until the war was over. It was after the war had ended that he got a call from one of the officers he had served with offering him a job at Gilbert Elliott and Co. in London's stock exchange. He agreed to join them more or less straight away and had been there ever since. He still got involved with his boxing, even taking control of local football clubs, a community hall near his flat, wrestling, cinema nights and bingo clubs. He was the sort of man who would turn up with a pair of football boots and start teaching the local kids how to play off his own back. A very honest man, over the years he became settled in his lifestyle and enjoyed his job. Ken would look up to his father over the years and eventually grow up to become one of the famous London black cab drivers and marry a girl called Lynda, and they would both set up home together in Ware, Hertfordshire. Over the years Ken would become an expert in the streets of London, knowing them like the back of his hand. Ken and Lynda would make Thomas and Frances proud in 1970 when they would give them their first granddaughter Claire.

Today Thomas was on his usual train heading into the City; sometimes Ken would save his dad the trip and go pick him up in his cab so he could chat to him along the way. Today Ken had a choice.... Should he pick up a fare or go and pick his dad up? He decided to pick up a customer and take a fare. It was a decision that would haunt him for the rest of his life.

*

Wearing a sari and a host of diamond rings, 26-year-old Bangladeshi student Shameen Banu Syed, was heading off to work to collect her things from her desk. Known by her family as Nargis, this was the last day she would be working at Pubali Bank in Finsbury Square as she was starting a new job at the Uttara Bank which was not far from where she normally went anyway. Born in Dhaka in 1949, she had already achieved her Masters degree in her home country, and it was in the early part of the 1970s that she met Tozammel Syed while he was temporarily in Dhaka. He had a BSc in engineering and had even worked for London Underground for the whole of 1970. Later taking a job with a pharmaceutical company, he was offered an engineering position in Bangladesh and that is where he met his future wife. They married on 9th June 1973 and planned their lives and careers, heading to London just over a year later in the August of 1974. Her mother had expressed sadness at seeing her daughter go away to a foreign land and although she would be missed, she was happy that Shameen was making something of her life. In one letter she wrote to her mother: "Amma! I will give you a surprise visit in March!" which gave her mother something to look forward to. Tozammel had lived in London many times but this was Shameen's first time in England, but she seemed to settle into the way of life and immediately applied for higher education at a university in order to study Bengali literature, hoping to finally get her PhD in the subject when she started class in September of 1975.

Living in a flat in Wood Green, she would head to the nearest tube station and board her usual train, changing at Finsbury Park and heading down to Moorgate, before continuing her journey on foot the rest of the way. Her husband would get up at around 0800, a little earlier than Shameen, as he had to be at his office at the General Electric Company in Borehamwood for 0900, whereas Shameen's work would open at 0930. The woman upstairs, also a Bengali woman named Sailla, worked at the same bank as Shameen and it was usual for them to head off to work together, but today she had accidentally slept in and would be late. Not to worry she would head off as normal and her neighbour would catch up with her soon. If she hurried up she would make it before the official opening. Shameen had a slight fever and Sailla offered to get her things for her from work to save her doing it, but she was keen to go in one last time herself and set off for Wood Street station.

Alistair Gordon in 1972   **Shameen Syed**

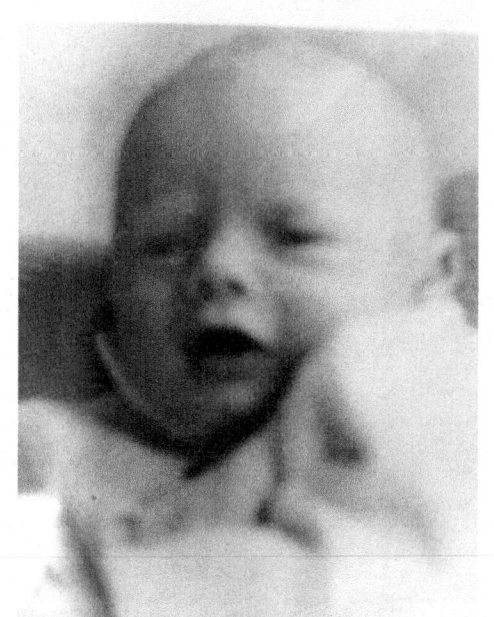

**One of the only photos of Antony Byczkowski as a baby.
As an adult he never liked his photo being taken.**

Barry Coppock (taken in 1981)

Javier Gonzalez in 1977   **Leslie Newson**

Leslie Newson 6th November 1943

Helen, Leslie and Sandra Newson

Les Newson's medals (photo by Robert Newson)

41

Helen and Leslie Newson - 2nd September 1974

Leslie Newson and grandson - early August 1974

Lesley, Terry (middle) and Frances Hall

Bernard Marks

Fred Wonderling

David Wilson - January 1975

43

George Mackmurdie wedding photo
1969

Janice Donovan

Jeff Benton

Stephen Payne

Thomas Thrower

Peter Bradbury 1972

Eileen Fleming (above left and right)

**Rosemarie Mansi, who was heading into the
City to attend her university courses**

Alan Francis (front left) and Alan Tibbenham (furthest left with the stripy tie) at Wood Street 1977 exchanging mementos with Lincs Constabulary

3. Disaster

As she stood in carriage one holding onto the bobble with her right hand, Marian King had decided to take out her book and was holding onto that with her free hand. As the train approached Moorgate she thought it was going unusually fast to say they were due to be stopping any moment. There seemed to be so many people in the carriage, most of them chatting away to each other about nothing in particular, but she was fine on her own with her novel. At the front of the same carriage stood police officer Margaret Liles getting ready to exit from the first set of doors and head up the escalators. Over in carriage five, Douglas Thomson realised too that the train was going much quicker than normal and suddenly the lights of the station illuminated the carriage with the MOORGATE signs flashing past. Barry Coppock looked up from his newspaper wondering what was going on, realising the train had entered the station but at considerable speed. In carriage one Jeff Benton and Margaret Liles had stood up ready to get off and were waiting at the doors; little did they know that one insignificant decision would alter the course of their lives. Just a few yards away from them, Javier Gonzalez also knew something wasn't right, he too realised that the train was going too fast and he looked up from his newspaper at the woman opposite. Almost everybody on the train was now wondering what was going on. The train should be coasting to a stop, especially with Les Newson at the controls. Guard Robert Harris had left his position at the rear to enter the carriage and look for a newspaper for him to read. By the time he realised they had entered the station at speed, the front of the train was just yards from an inevitable collision. Few people on board were aware that the line ended at Moorgate; the tunnel ahead was just for slight over-runs before it ended abruptly at a solid brick wall.

The people in the station waiting on the platform were shocked to see the speed at which the train was coming in. With no sound of the brakes being applied it was obvious that something bad was about to happen and nobody could do a thing about it. Those on the train had little time to react to pull the emergency brakes, even if they did it would not have much effect. After it entered the station out of the tunnel, it took just nine seconds for the front carriage of the train to reach the end of the platform. According to several people they caught a glimpse of motorman Les Newson sat in his seat upright, staring straight ahead, before disappearing into the overshoot tunnel. The time was 0846.

In the split second the front bogey mounted the sand drag it propelled the train at an angle where the driver's cab slammed into the wall near the roof at around 35mph, crumpling the first carriage and forcing it into a V-shape. Marian was thrown forward and immediately lost consciousness. In that same split second the sand had operated an emergency brake on the outside of the wheels, being instantly reset by the pulling of the reset cord when it detached from the bottom of the carriage. Pushing the crumpled car into its V-shape was the momentum that was carriage two – this had dug its way under carriage one and again telescoped into almost half its length. With the thrusting and energy of the movement still not over, carriage three tried to find a space above carriage two leaving the front half of it wedged between the roof of car two and the ceiling. In just a few seconds the train had come to a halt and rested where it lay, incredibly the back three cars being completely undamaged.

At the moment of impact Doug had been thrown out of his seat and grabbed out at something to stop him flying off, unfortunately it was the throat of the man sat opposite. His friend Jim tried running to the other end to find a way out but he was accidentally tripped up. Barry Coppock was thrown sideways over the seat rest after feeling three to four hard shudders, but believing that the driver had slammed the brakes on at the last second. Javier Gonzalez in carriage one recalls today, "An almighty sound, like an explosion, twisting metal and glass breaking, no one shouted, nor cried, everything happened in a fraction of a second, the time it takes you to inhale air into your lungs when breathing."

*

With a sense of silent shock the doors finally opened on the back half of the train after a short delay. Barry got out of the carriage and headed away from the train to walk to the escalator, but he was halted by a huge cloud of dust that was enveloping the front carriages. Not realising what had just actually happened he noticed the exit that led onto platform 10 and out of the station. There was no way he would walk through all that dirt, he would be filthy by the time he reached work. He glanced around and headed a few yards to the rear exit and out. There were no cries for help or any screaming so it must have just been a sudden braking, he remembers thinking. Running up the stairs he exited into the street and headed off to his work.

Not in a million years did he think he had just walked away from a major disaster.

Nearby, Douglas and Jim also exited and headed towards the front of the train where they could see the dust and smoke. At this point they thought there was an immediate danger of fire and were quite worried for all those still on board. But as they got closer they realised it wasn't actually smoke, it was red-brown dust that had been thrown about from inside the tunnel. Douglas noticed that the silence was "very weird" as he looked at the carriages. The train was sticking out of the over-run tunnel at an angle and suddenly a woman came out of the carriage. Wearing a red dress and having a black face from the soot, her mouth gaping open, another came out talking already of compensation for her damaged clothes. It was so quiet that he was sure that everybody in the first half of the train was dead. He needed to get out of there quick before the train caught fire. Nearby was the man who he had accidentally strangled in the carriage, standing up against the wall rubbing his neck. As other people on the platform began by calling the emergency services and setting up a rescue centre, Douglas went up the escalator, he needed to sit down. He exited the station and found a nearby coffee shop and slowly drank his coffee, shaking at the sight that befell him just moments ago. Although there was nothing he could do to recover anybody from the tunnel he felt a huge amount of guilt for leaving them. It was then Jim turned to him and said, "Doug...you were in the front carriage but you left it and went further back." It suddenly dawned on him just how lucky he had been. It also dawned on him that his friend Jeff had stayed. He was clearly in shock although he didn't think about it at the time.

*

Up at street level Barry Coppock had arrived at work early as usual, well ahead of the rush of people. With a bit of time to spare he went into a local café for a cup of tea, he would be starting work around fifteen minutes later. Suddenly he started seeing police cars and ambulances turn up. People were coming into the café and talking about a crash at the station. He mentioned to one of them that it was only an over-run and apart from probably a few people knocking themselves they would be fine. What he didn't know, like many others, was that there was a brick wall at the end of the line. The arriving ambulances, although normal for any incident of this nature, would soon be bringing out more than just a few bumps and bruises. In fact people were already staggering out of the carriages, bleeding, lungs full of dust, hair and clothes covered in soot. These were the lucky ones. Trapped in the front carriages were those who were unconscious, alive but unable to move, trapped with those that were dead. For these people, the horror had only just begun.

4. Trapped in the Darkness

The first calls started to hit London's emergency services within seconds of the crash. All over the city bells were ringing for police, fire and ambulance to hurry to the scene. The scale of the disaster was unknown at this time but one thing was sure, with the speed at which the train had hit the wall, it was a guarantee that there would be mass casualties and fatalities.

At police HQ at Old Jury, Brian Fisher was just getting changed into his uniform after getting off the tube. He got a phone call from the control centre who told him that there had been a rail crash at Moorgate station, he immediately told them to have his disaster action plan put into force and he rushed off to speak to the commissioner to brief him. All that planning and exercising for disaster was about to be put into action. After quickly telling him what the score was, Brian Fisher headed off to the crash site, being one of the first police officers on scene, arriving just before 9am, only minutes after the initial crash. As he arrived he saw that there were not many people around yet; one of those already on scene told him what had happened and what had been found out so far, he worked out for himself where to head with the situation from then on. As senior officer and master of disaster planning, he was now officially in charge of this incident. He knew what was happening, what was not on site, what needed to be on site. It would be another half hour after the crash that he could actually make his way down to the platform to see for himself the scene of the disaster, once he had coordinated his teams on the surface. These were the same people who he had trained with to coordinate his disaster plan. Everybody knew what to do, everybody knew where they had to be, everybody had their positions.

Inspector Brian Tibbenham had been in the City of London police for eighteen years and enjoyed his job. He was responsible for the cover of the streets; usually around five inspectors would do this in different shifts with three sergeants and ten to fifteen constables under them. He had been on duty at the Wood Street station front office when somebody came in and told him of the unfolding events round the corner. He had only just come on shift, working a usual nine to five, and had literally just put his uniform on. He and his colleague Jim Thompson made their way out of the station and down London Wall round to the scene, Brian staying at street level and Jim going below to see what the situation was. Jim had been one of the first on the scene being a street cop and was in the middle of a patrol walk when the call had come in. As Brian Tibbenham was taking charge of the PCs on the street level, Brian Fisher had just turned up himself to take charge of the entire scene. At this point police, fire brigade and ambulances started turning up. He decided to stay out of the way and let the firefighters do their job; having a policeman in the way would only hinder their job of rescuing whoever was down there. But suddenly he was thrust into the job of being press liaison officer; he now had to talk to the TV and newspaper reporters and be very careful to control what was being said and what information they knew for sure.

At around 9am the London Ambulance Service asked St Bart's Hospital to send a doctor to the site; a casualty officer left immediately with a medical student and a small first aid bag. On assessment of the situation on scene they called for a resuscitation team which left at around 0920. Slowly but surely word was getting out of the major incident that was occurring underground. However, the scale of the incident was still unknown. The eventual realisation of what was going on in the short tunnel over-run would shock everybody.

*

By now more survivors were making their way out of the train. The lucky ones could walk up the escalator unaided, coming face to face with the first police officers. The amount of dirt and soot on their faces and clothes, together with a dazed look on many of them, led to their being escorted out and placed into the back of the first waiting ambulances. Still with the notion that they were dealing with cuts and bruises, the rescue teams hurried down to platform 9.

All around London the fire stations were alive with the sense of urgency as calls were coming in thick and fast. The scale of the disaster was increasing by the minute and to this end, fire crews were kitting up and racing to the scene. One of these firemen was Frank David, a 32-year-old station officer at Brigade HQ in Lambeth. He had been in the service eleven years and that morning had not long been in the office when his boss Charles Clisby came in and said, "There has been a horrendous crash at the Underground in Moorgate!" A new communications tool had only recently been developed called FIGARO – the Fire Ground Apparatus Radio comms – and this was developed for exactly this type of job. Today it would be needed more than anything else. Being in charge of the communications equipment and radios, he packed up the FIGARO systems into the department's Land rover and sped to the scene of the crash.

Over in the East End of London at Silvertown was station officer Norman "Nap" Paulding. He had joined the London Fire Brigade in 1959 after doing his national service in the Royal Corps of Signals, spending a fair amount of time in Malaya during the Korean War, leaving his army life in 1953. He had arrived for duty that morning at 9am and immediately heard about the events in the City through the teleprinters as messages were being sent from the control station to all other stations. Because the station was around twenty minutes drive time away, it was decided to allow the fire crews closer to the scene to attend and deal with it; they would be on hand if they needed any further help.

Twenty-three year old PC Gary Thomas had been in the police for seven years, officially becoming a constable in 1971, being now based at Snow Hill station. At the time he was living above Wood Street station as there were no beds in the single quarters so he had to live there for the time being. Suddenly he heard a call come over the radio: *"Any unit near Moorgate, we got a report of a train gone into the buffers."* He immediately headed down the road and as he approached the station entrance he saw that it was remarkably calm, people were acting like nothing had happened, nobody saying a word, people coming up the escalator as normal (bearing in mind the crash had just happened and trains were still bringing passengers on the other three lines every few minutes). Gary proceeded down to platform 9 and saw a London Underground supervisor stood on the platform in a trance, the scene looked normal and OK at first glance.

Questions were flying around all those who first stepped onto the platform – there seemed to be only four carriages. Where were the rest of them? Not realising that there was a wall at the end of tunnel, many people instantly played down the scale of what was happening. Although it was a major incident, nobody yet could tell just how bad it was. Gary headed back to street level to let the fire crews do their job and he began directing people down to the platform before passing control down to the supervisor.

Fireman Frank David had begun to set his equipment up at street level and headed down to the crash. Wearing the FIGARO set he did a comms check below the street and found that it worked better than he had hoped. The headset was worn over his head with an aerial sown into the edge of a waistcoat. Approaching the scene he saw a lot of dirt and dust still in the air that had been stirred up, it looked like an explosion had taken place, although at the moment breathing wasn't an issue; it was more "murky" than a difficulty. This was now the first time this new communications system had been used in a real life operation. Walkie-talkies were no use down there so he would be the man who would relay the information back up to street level and give the regular reports. He boarded carriage three and was amazed to find it still working without a problem. For something like this it was perfect, for tackling a blaze it would be more of a hindrance and inconvenient. With the first rescue teams on scene, the operation could now officially begin.

*

That Friday would propel 26-year-old Times journalist Laurence Marks in a completely different direction. He sat at his desk and pressed the talking clock. *"Oh eight fifty-three...and twenty seconds. Bip. Bip. Bip."* Seconds later the phone rang and he recognised the voice straight away as that of the day editor. "There is an incident at Moorgate Underground, there is no more information, it seems to have run over." With this small amount of detail he set off to cover the story. Knowing the tube map like the back of his hand he took a journey across London to collect his notebook and other bits he would need before getting to Liverpool Street station just after 10am. By this time there were a number of fire engines, police cars, sirens, blue lights, ambulances with their doors open and police motorcycles keeping the routes to the hospitals clear. The entire area was cordoned off by the City of London police, but one flash of his press card allowed him to continue towards the news crew area that had now started growing as the scale of the incident was becoming more apparent.

He could hear them referring to the crash as a major incident; it must be bad! This was going to be on every news placard around London, possibly the country. He started wondering what the incident was; one colleague speculating IRA involvement, with nothing being officially told, yet rumours were rife with guesses and any one of them was as good as the rest.

It was when the train's passengers were coming out of the station entrance covered in soot and being ushered into the backs of the ambulances that they asked the advice of a London Transport employee who was nearby.

"A train's gone through the buffers, many injuries," he said.
"Any dead?"
"Don't know yet."

Laurence knew this was front page stuff! More and more ambulances were arriving, more survivors of this incident were being brought up to the sound of a photographer's camera going off. He looked at them as they were being led away thinking that they could be mistaken for miners coming out of a coal pit after a hard day at work. Only the dirty white shirts and ties gave it away that these were office workers heading into the City. A police officer from the City forces then informed the press that a six-carriage train on the Northern-City Line had overshot the buffers but that was all the information they were able to release for the time being.

A little while later Brian Tibbenham would gather the reporters together and say, "I can't take you all down, you lot have to nominate one person to see and hear everything for you and to share it," to which they all agreed.

*

Tim Hatton was a 23-year-old leading firefighter for the London Fire Brigade who had joined the service in 1972. Based at Clapham Old Town Street (now closed down), he worked there but actually lived above Brixton fire station. At around 9am he was turned out to stand by at Westminster, as their firefighters had already been dispatched to Moorgate, and moved out straight away. On the way to Westminster they were mobilised straight to the scene of the crash. *"Proceed to incident at Moorgate tube station,"* said the order. Normally you check all equipment before a shift start but this time they didn't even have chance to do that before they were sent straight out with a crew of five on their Dennis F14 truck complete with pump escape.

They arrived at around 0945, although they were not the first to arrive as there were already several there, but they were still ahead of most of the others that had already been mobilised around London. They parked within 150 yards of the entrance down a side road and exited the truck. The fire group was split up; one of the guys was suddenly convinced his girlfriend was on the train so he wasn't seen for a while as he had disappeared. (He would turn up several hours later when he knew she was OK and not involved.) The rest of them stuck together and hung about waiting to be told what the situation was and what assistance they could provide. They made their way down the stairs and down the escalators to the scene of the incident; at one point standing on the platform, Tim said it looked more like a film set. He described the images that greeted him as "controlled chaos" with lots of people standing around as the majority of the work was being conducted in the tunnel away from the eyes of those nearby. There were a lot of senior officers turning up at the site, with it now being such a big event.

Some of the teams had gone into the tunnel and managed to squeeze down the side of the train deep into the darkness. People were just doing what they could. By this time around 100 firemen were down at the scene, the only ones who could do anything were those cutting away at the wreckage squeezed into the narrow spaces. Tim went down the side of the train as far as he could go, by now they had started removing the bodies of the victims, bringing them down the side as well as through the train carriages. They formed a line between the tunnel and train and slid them along in a chain to the platform. He noticed the body of a young girl laid in silence with her hand flopped out, wearing what looked like a wedding ring, Tim thinking, "She probably hasn't been married long, she will never be going home." Knowing that this was most likely a multiple fatality incident he prepared himself for the tasks ahead. The teams were working extremely hard in the heat and the cramped spaces, but still giving a lot of respect to those who were obviously deceased.

*

Blue Watch fireman Brian Goodfellow had just turned up for work when at 0858 the lads were gathering together, both the oncoming and off-going duty crews being mustered as part of the daily handover of responsibility. He was nicknamed "Freezer" (as in freezer-jolly-good-fellow) and he had already seen his fair share of big jobs. Since joining the London Fire Brigade on 1st June 1970 he had attended the 1972 Staines air disaster (the same crash that Brian Fisher had attended with his emergency planning teams).

Normally when a call came through for a job they would go through to the "Duty Box" where right now they would ring six bells for the role call before testing the bells. Getting ready for the morning muster the bells went, leading to the men laughing in the belief that the duty man had wrung the wrong bell, until he ran in with a call slip.

"Ah you've messed up!" they shouted

"No! A train's hit the buffers! It's a shout!"

With their faces suddenly realising the severity of what he was saying, they quickly gathered their equipment together, Brian jumped in the driving seat of the emergency tender with five others climbing aboard. This truck would carry the rescue gear, not a pump machine like a regular fire engine, but cutting gear, hydraulic jacks, chocks and hand tools, amongst other heavy kit. Normally a shout on the London Underground network would be for a suicide, known by the fire teams as a "one under", so they had had good training to deal with these and other accidents. On top of this they were highly trained, with harder and harder exercises designed to deal with more complicated situations, and would be back-up team to those on breathing apparatus.

Apart from an argument with a man who had parked in their way, they raced across London in full firefighting gear, parking the fire "bus" outside the station entrance on the main road. They blocked the street off on that side, leaving the bus which would stay there until completion of the job in hand and would be the equipment dump for the teams.

Brian and his team seemed to be amongst the first there as it was pretty much devoid of any emergency vehicles. They had got there fast enough due to pretty light traffic, while people were still exiting the station from other trains, unaware of the drama unfolding beneath their feet. Other pedestrians were being directed away from the pavement outside and prevented from going in the station to give rescuers free access to the station without having to struggle.

Without really knowing what awaited them, they grabbed as much of the kit as possible and headed down to platform 9, going in three side-by-side carrying the heavy equipment in between, joining the firemen together like a tidal surge sweeping the pavement. People were still coming up the stairs "looking like pandas...or black and white minstrels, with white lips and eyes". Racing up the stairs behind them was a fireman from the Barbican who stopped them. "The guv'nor's making it major incident procedure!"

This meant that the shout was now escalated, that somewhere below was an incident where you have a minimum of thirty injuries, people who cannot move and others that need immediate assistance. There are three types of people in a triangle: the movable who need assistance, the injured who can help themselves (self-assisted) and those who are trapped and/or injured. At this point the call was going out to all hospitals to stand by for multiple casualties, to the ambulances to bring medical teams, the police to help with the roads being congested, fire brigade command units, Salvation Army and many more.

As the teams entered the scene, people were being taken off the back of the train and shepherded onto platform 10 and away from the carnage that awaited Brian. First thing was to set up an equipment dump down on the ground; looking around it didn't seem as bad as they thought. The train was slightly angled but nothing like what they were expecting. This came as a relief, maybe it would be just cuts and bruises – the odd person having to be cut out. With a bit of luck they would have it all wrapped up in no time! They were standing just a few yards away from the driver's cab, not realising that what they thought held the driver was actually carriage three.

*

Adrian Eatwell and Tony Wallis worked for the City of London photography section as part of the investigation teams. Tony had joined the police in July 1969 and went into the photography department four years later, completing the course in March 1974 at Hendon. Adrian was due to come to work at Snow Hill at 9am when, as he was crossing the road, he heard the sirens of ambulances and the senior officer's car. He went straight to work to find out what was going on, and as soon as he walked through the door he could hear the phones going out of control, talk in the air of an accident at Moorgate station. Grabbing their kit together, Adrian and Tony got the duty car to pick them up and raced over to the station and arrived just minutes later. Expecting it to be just a slight bump of one train going into another, they realised that something was not right when they entered the station at the Britannic House entrance and made their way onto platform 9 to find that two expected carriages were missing. Their job would start once the rescue phase had ended, until then it was a case of making themselves useful where they could, photographing anything and everything in case it was relevant to what would be a huge investigation process.

They had arrived on scene pretty quickly and by now more were turning up. Survivors had already been carried out of the carriages carefully and laid on the platform where emergency doctors who had raced from St Bart's Hospital would tend to any wounds. Platform 10 was used as a base to take them out of the area so they wouldn't have to be in the way of the other firemen and could be left alone to do their work.

Another photographer was Andy Day who had already been involved in many other major incidents in London such as the IRA bombings at the Old Bailey, Finsbury Circus and the Stock Exchange. He had joined the police in 1961 as a cadet and rose to detective constable in 1975. Again he was part of the investigation team so he too had to take a step back and photograph things that would not get in the way of the rescuers. His work would be collected over time as part of what would obviously be a massive inquiry.

*

Marian King woke up in pitch darkness in a state of confusion. Getting her thoughts together she realised that she had to get up for work or she would be late. But something didn't feel right. Then it suddenly dawned on her…. She had done all that already, what was going on? As her hazy thoughts were becoming clearer she realised that something was wrong. She was trapped on the train, the underground was the last thing she remembered. She must still be on it, had something bad happened? As she was casting her mind back through the last few hours, she was suddenly aware that she was not alone. Thanks to the lighter clothes she had worn for work the heat was just bearable (for now), but it was already getting hot. What sounded like a Scottish accent then called out to her. "I think there's been an accident!" he said. They both seemed comfortable enough, not in any pain or distress, just caught up and unable to free themselves. At this point she was glad that she was travelling alone, she would not want her family to be where she was now! She doesn't remember the initial impact which means she had lost consciousness immediately, and feeling a bit drowsy still she was just in time to see the yellow tinge of some light of a firefighter before she slipped into unconsciousness again.

Just a few feet away in carriage one was WPC Margaret Liles. She couldn't move as, like Marian, she was trapped. She couldn't feel her left foot. There were cries for help, and shouting erupted for a brief moment as somebody decided it would be a good idea to light a match. She felt like she was slightly sitting on something although she was still standing. Realising it was a person, she was in a situation now where if *she* moved it would hurt *them*, and if *they* moved it hurt *her*. Realising that the only way to avoid any pain was to stay still, they both settled where they were as best they could. This man she was entangled with was Jeff Benton.

Confusion reigned in all the people still alive in the tunnel. Margaret was convinced that the train had hit the buffer and very soon the passengers would disembark from the rear and they would all walk out. As reality was sinking in, it soon became apparent that this was more than just a shunting of the buffers. Jeff and Margaret began talking to each other.

"You sound very young" he said. "You sound very young and you are being very brave."

"Well I am a policewoman now, I must be brave."

Jeff then shouted out that everything would be alright as there was a policewoman here. In the pitch black she couldn't make out anything at all, time had stood still yet there was no panic. Thankfully the darkness was shielding them from the awful sight that was around them.

*

Within half an hour of the disaster the Red Cross were mobilized and twenty of the crew turned up at the scene to be allocated various duties by the police. Their jobs were mostly helping comfort the survivors and later to help the bereaved relatives. They helped to set up the canteens and usher people towards the blood donation centres that were soon being set up.

At 0940 the alert sounded at the Salvation Army's Hoxton Goodwill Centre which had Captain Joe Burlison and his team heading down to the disaster. Burlison had had experience with critical situations having previously been a member of a mine rescue team. When the police informed him of what was happening in the City, they opened up a mobile canteen near the station entrance to supply the emergency services with refreshments, initially being done by the City of London Polytechnic, ironically where Javier Gonzalez was heading that morning. Officers were sent to the three hospitals where the survivors were being treated – Guys, Bart's and the London.

The ground floor of the nearby thirty-five storey BP building, named Britannic House, was now opened up by the owners as a centre for donating blood. Supplies of blood from the blood banks were rushed to the hospitals with any spare doctors, but this was not enough. Nurses from the National Blood Service took their place and before long queues were forming out into the street to donate. Police officers announced it through a loud hailer outside Moorgate station calling for anybody willing to give blood, and many people rushed off to do so. One hundred yards from Moorgate station, at one point, the queue peaked at 2,000: students abandoned a protest rally to give blood, a Portuguese café worker plied staff with free coffee and doughnuts, while taxi drivers offered free lifts to anybody who wanted to give blood. The restaurant in the BP building also opened up for the emergency crews to eat in between working.

As all this voluntary work was being noticed, a local office party decided to send down their cakes to give to the rescuers to give them something to eat and keep their energy up, most of whom would just be drinking all day and not eat anything until they realised it had been several hours since their last meal. Even a boy scout came down to lend a hand. But it wasn't just serving tea and cake that those on the scene were doing. Some were helping survivors out of the station and some even carried out the grim task of helping carry out the bodies of the dead. The Salvation Army would remain there until midday on the following Wednesday 5th March. It was estimated that around sixty to seventy officers were on the scene, their selfless acts being noted by the press and appreciated especially by the rescue teams.

*

Brian Goodfellow and his fire-fighting team were now inside carriage three, still unaware that they were at the back of the third carriage. Trapped in a seat was a young woman, around eighteen to twenty years old, with a lump of metal in her leg. She was obviously in shock so he began chatting to her to make sure she kept awake and coherent. He needed to get her talking back to him so he began a random conversation while they rigged the cutting equipment. "What are you doing this weekend?" he asked, undoing her jacket to free her trapped shoulder. She was in a lot of pain as the air cutter "senger saw" chewed through the metal leaving a chunk still in her leg for the doctors to deal with once she was out. The vibrations couldn't be helped but that still didn't stop her crying out in agony. In a few minutes the task was over and she was stretchered out of the train and up the escalator. As she left the scene, Brian shouted back to her, "Don't forget we've made a date! We'll see you at the disco Saturday night!"

By now the heat was starting to build up, they were wearing bulky clothing and after all the hard work so far carrying the kit and struggling to free the young woman they would soon so very easily become exhausted. The torch they carried was also getting annoying (as usual). It was known as a Bardic torch, or safety lamp, which was intrinsically safe to use without causing a spark when attending a scene. The fire teams would nickname this the "knacker-knocker" due to it being placed on the belts and constantly banging them in the crotch when working! But they should be finished soon, the driver was just on the other side of the bulkhead...or so they thought.

Other fire crews had by now made their way down the side of the train and, dropping down low, had crawled along and come across a pile of sand and dirt. They heard lots of shouting from above; looking up and seeing the train's bogeys above their heads was not what they expected. This was now very confusing... where had this come from? What exactly were they looking at? What had happened here? Counting the wheels sticking out of the wreckage it suddenly dawned on them.... "Hang on...that's another carriage!" shouted a fireman.

Brian had slid down the side and tried to get into the front from below. He saw another door and what looked like a body, so began to climb upwards, the men having to put their boots wherever they could in order to step up to get into carriage two, though again they believed that this now was the driver's cab. In total darkness with nothing but a flashlight to guide them, Brian saw people littering the wrecked carriage, a woman with auburn hair moaning (though this could have been blood from a head injury). "Don't worry, we're here now," he said to her, hoping it would rouse her or some others to call back to him. Other people were behind her, looking like they had slid down the centre aisle. In an uncomfortable pile meeting in the middle, they seemed to be compressed together, on top of one another, sitting still in seats. Those at the bottom of the piles were trapped by the sheer weight of those above them. One of those sat bolt upright was clearly dead; looking peaceful, a man in a suit with clear military bearing sat with several others. It was incredible how so much could have happened around them yet they stayed perfectly still, like they were just waiting to come into the station before standing up to get off. Due to the huge number of people needing attention, both dead and alive, it was necessary for them to give random names to them in order for easy identification by others. Brian named this unknown victim "The City Gent". He would later be formally identified as Bernard Marks.

*

Another fire crew were now joining Brian's team and they got together to work out a plan to recover the driver, making their way out of the carriage and back into the tunnel. Squeezing out into the blackness, he looked up and saw another wheel on the roof as he shone his torch up. A body hung down through the wreckage and they stared in disbelief. "What carriage is this then?" they said confused. It suddenly dawned on them that yet another carriage lay above them, twisted and unrecognisable. Shining their lights around, they located a single door and forced it open. By now it had dawned on everybody working in the tunnel that two full carriages were compressed together and somehow squashed into this short over-run. At morning rush hour, this could only mean that the seriousness of the situation was now off the scale. Realising the enormity of the task ahead, they proceeded to enter the first carriage.

By now they realised that what they had just gone through in carriage two was now duplicated in this new carriage, but with more horrors to come. Brian entered with one other member of his team, carrying a hacksaw over his shoulder, the rest of the crew still working in carriage two. This seemed to be at a steeper angle and he was looking down into the unknown, everything seeming black, at a forty-five degree angle looking like you would fall downwards into it. By this point they were both exhausted and coming close to their limit, but they continued on in the hope of securing the scene and identifying any survivors. They could hear other people calling out, but with just two of them able to get to them, it was decided that Brian would stay in carriage one alone for the few minutes it would take for his partner to summon further assistance with the tasks. Brian was then left to stare down into carriage one, a scene of utter carnage, the entire length twisted in half to form a V-shape, the back section looking like a straight drop. He began climbing down using the chairs as a ladder, everything at the back thrown forward to pile up in the middle of the V.

Looking further down he saw a lump of curved metal with people behind it, it obviously needed to be sawn off. The task ahead was immense and he was now alone in carriage one with nothing but a flashlight to guide him. Alone in the carriage, he suddenly felt very nervous.

*

Ambulanceman Dave Tovey had joined the Surrey ambulance service in 1961, coming over to London a year later. He wasn't aware of the Moorgate crash until he arrived back at the HQ training school where he was responsible for the training of ambulance cadets and had just taken them to college for their day release education. As he arrived back he was told immediately of the situation at Moorgate and to head over there in an ambulance with oxygen supplies. He dashed to the crash site and reported to the Incident Officer who asked him to pick up a medical team from the London Hospital in Whitechapel. He raced through the streets to carry out his task and after delivering his precious cargo, he was instructed to head down to the platform and see if any of the other crews needed to be ferried back to HQ in an ambulance car for a break. It was revealed that a breakdown in communications meant that the correct information was not getting from the scene to the hospitals, but that did not impede the care that was given to the patients nor did it delay any of the treatment that was received by them. A medical post was established in the middle of carriage two in order to check over for vital signs of casualties, strapped to Neil Robertson stretchers. The emergency resuscitation area on platform 10 was set up soon after 10am by doctors from the London Hospital. Back-up was called and soon eleven doctors arrived with seven extra nurses.

*

Shining his torch into the blackness of carriage one, fireman Brian Goodfellow suddenly saw a sea of faces looking up at him. He shouted down, "Don't worry...we're here!" but wasn't sure if he heard anybody reply. The twisted metal that was holding people down was the first of many obvious problems so he set to work on removing it, still on his own. Taking his hack saw off his shoulder he began sawing away at the metal.

Suddenly he felt hands appear out of nowhere and grab hold of him. Like a scene out of a horror movie, he was being held down by a flurry of hands pulling him back. He started to feel very anxious as the people down here could see him yet he couldn't see them. The hands were talking to him in silent voices, as if to say *"you got in here... if you go out again you are taking me with you!"*

He felt an urge to get out of there as quickly as possible as his heart started racing, taking on a drowning sensation as he unfastened his fire jacket and let it drop, escaping from the hands that were pulling him down into their hell. He had already been working for a long time and he would have been overdue a break despite his enthusiasm to continue working to get the people out.

In what seemed like an eternity, but was probably only a minute or two, his colleague returned with more firemen to help. Brian looked at him and simply said, "I need a break," before scurrying out of the carriage, down the side of the train and onto the platform. His emotions were everywhere by now. He felt panic at the thought of being trapped in the wreckage, death and destruction all around him. He felt guilt at leaving those trapped (even though the other men were on it now). Most of all he felt utterly exhausted and was in visible shock. People stopped to ask him if he was OK as he sat down on the platform, but he just told them to leave him alone which they did. He sat at the equipment dump alone with his thoughts.

*

For Javier Gonzalez, a strange phenomenon now became apparent. He could not tell whether it was his imagination or reality. He was floating towards a peaceful white space in the air. He felt happy as he was away from the disaster now, he was away from people and in what he could only describe as heaven. Then suddenly he was catapulted back down to a place of hell, full of tortured screams in complete darkness and heat. Was he now dead and this was where he was going? These experiences were broken by a voice shouting down to him, "Is there anybody else there?" to which the shouter was met with only silence.

He gathered his strength together just to be able to shout back, "YES!! I am here!!"

"Can you move?" replied the voice.

Trying to move himself he then realised that he was face down on the carriage floor with his hands next to his shoulders. He was still not all that with it, but he had the sense to shout back, "No...I cannot move!" as he struggled with pain in his chest. The voice then told him to cover his face, which he obliged the best he could by putting his hands behind his head. He felt a needle go into the back of his hand and then his body was being raised up from his armpits.

"What is your name?" said Javier.

"My name is David," he replied.

"David, who are you?" he said back confused.

"I work for the rescue services," he said.

"Thank you, David," he said back, relieved that he now understood what was happening to him.

"Mind his back...and I think his leg is broken," shouted David to another team member. The second man passed him down to a third one. He kept repeating what the fireman had said about his injury just in case he hadn't heard. He didn't actually feel anything (most likely due to the fact that morphine was being injected into the survivors so they didn't feel the pain of their injuries during the struggle to extract them from the wreckage). He was then taken up to the surface and placed in an ambulance.

*

Soon after getting his breath back and calming down, Brian Goodfellow sat on the platform looking all around him at the scene. It felt as if everything was slowing down, that he was watching the entire incident being played out in slow motion. He noticed a man standing by the escalator, the rescue teams trying to lead him away. He was refusing to leave shouting, *"I'm not going until I've seen my wife!"* It seemed to him that he was an injured passenger who had had no news of his wife since the crash and feared the worst.

But then a woman emerged from the train, walking on her own but being supported. As she came round the corner and caught sight of the man, the sense of relief was so obvious, a joyful reunion on the brink of death. Together they were taken up the escalator.

Suddenly Brian's thoughts came back to the present, the noise started again and everything proceeded at normal pace. "It was as if I had been given a sudden slap," he would recall nearly forty years later. He was back to reality and ready to go back to work.

Heading back down the tunnel sides to carriage one, he crawled onto the roof where by now a hole had been made in the middle of the V so people could be hoisted out when they had been freed. It was obvious that there were several people trapped in this area; a man was heard shouting up, "Get me out! All you gotta do is get these people of my legs!" to which the firemen had to have a go at him to get him to shut up. If it had been as simple as just removing people then the job would have been finished hours ago. Next to him was what Brian saw as a "portly woman", who turned out to be passenger Eileen Smith.

Eileen had no memory of what happened and woke up to the sound of moaning. She suddenly started screaming as she thought she was in some kind of nightmare. A man's voice in the darkness persuaded her to calm down, that this was real and that help was on its way. He asked her name and that of a woman next to her. She recalled that she thinks the woman said Angela but couldn't be sure. He then asked if she was going on holiday this year. What a strange thing to be talking about in this situation, she thought. It was only later she realised why this voice was asking random questions. This same voice had also asked others trapped if they had any plans for the weekend or if they liked dancing. Before long she recognised that the fire teams had reached her.

"I often think of this man and would like to thank him from the bottom of my heart for keeping us both occupied until help came so we didn't have to dwell on the situation." (She would meet Brian thirty-nine years later after the author realised that their stories matched up. Needless to say it was an emotional reunion.) Eileen's brother had been a fireman so she had it in her head at the time that it was he who had come to get her out. By removing her, this would make space, but they had no idea who, if anybody, was trapped underneath her. They lowered a rope and got it attached around her waist, the firemen taking up the strain and ready to pull her out through the rear of the carriage. She was talking to them but not really listening to them. She complained about the pain in her legs, shoulder and around her ribs. There was no way to avoid hurting her as they planned to get her out. Two others including "Angela" were hoisted out first before they could get to Eileen.

It became apparent that Eileen's leg was still trapped and Brian had to run his hand down to find what it was that was stopping her moving. She was then laid on her back and pulled at a forty-five degree angle on the train floor, being pushed from below. Putting her right hand up to help as much as she could she cried out in pain, her left hand and arm stretching up to her shoulder in agony, shouting a line of obscenities, much to her later embarrassment. Thankfully she was grabbed by the firemen and slowly pulled towards the opening until she reached the back of the carriage and was hoisted out. She was taken down the platform and offered a wheelchair. She refused this as she had walked onto the train and was determined to walk out, even if she did need a little help. Two men helped her up the escalators to a waiting ambulance where a photographer captured the moment on camera as she emerged from the station stairs.

The first thing she asked for was water, but as they didn't have any cups available she was given a bucket full of water before being put on oxygen as she was having difficulty breathing still. The ambulance took her to the London Hospital where she was found to have two fractured ribs, a collapsed lung, a fractured shoulder blade, and cuts and bruises to both legs. It became apparent that she shouldn't have had the water as they had to do an emergency procedure on her immediately to get a drain into her lungs as there was so much soot in them; she had been constantly breathing it in while trapped down the tunnel for several hours. They could do nothing about the ribs because of the shoulder blade and could do nothing about the shoulder blades because of the ribs. She had to live very carefully from now on, at least until they healed properly. Although the cuts and bruises on her leg would heal, the muscle at the top of her left leg later dropped and she had to have an operation on her right leg.

*

Heading back down into the bottom of the V, Brian started falling on top of people and had to lay across one load of people in order to get to others, such was the tangled mess of people and metal that was there. He had a safety line around him but that would do very little for this task. Flashing the torch around a hand suddenly came out, and a very polite female voice said, "Excuse me, could I have some water please?"

They thought, "How are we going to get water?"

"We'll sort you out," they said

"Thank you," she replied.

Pulling the bodies back, they did everything they could to minimise further injury; it was like a puzzle trying to free people. The fire crews worked well as a team, forming a chain when survivors had to be passed down and equipment had to be passed back up. In the tragedy and confusion of the crash, doctors asked for a bottle of entonox. However, because of the word being passed down and getting mixed up along the way, a cardboard box was sent back up. Looking confused, the doctor simply said, "What the f..k is this?"

"You asked for an empty box."

"I want entonox! Gas and air!"

"You'll probably get a cuddly bear," remarked the fireman

sarcastically, as the order was relayed. In such a situation it is very easy for mis-communication between groups of people.

Looking around the carriage, still full of trapped people, both dead and alive, Brian noticed a body with a huge wristwatch on. It was apparent that, judging by the number of nicknames they had been having to give the victims to aid each other – the City Gent, the Girl with the auburn hair, man with large wristwatch – it was obvious by now that they were dealing with many fatalities.

At 4pm that afternoon he was relieved, he was off watch anyway at 6pm but by now he had been down there from when the call came in around 9am – seven hours in total struggling with the heat, dust, dirt, bodies and the heavy tasks involved. He made his way to street level where he was picked up in a different vehicle to what he came in, as his mobile unit had to remain on scene, heading back to Clerkenwell fire station. When he arrived there, the standby crews wanted to know everything that had happened as they had only heard what was already known over the air and radios, but nobody wanted to talk about it. They felt like they had a constant dry taste in their mouths, covered as they were in dirt and dust, and so couldn't stop cleaning their teeth. If only the memories of what they saw could be washed away so easily.

*

Back in the stifling heat of the tunnel, Margaret Liles felt a sudden draught of air followed by a faint glimmer of torchlight. Noises of people using tools, voices and clambering about could now be heard as the rescuers were closing in on them inch by inch. The torchlight got brighter and Jeff Benton shouted out that he was alive. "And me!" said Margaret, not convinced that anybody could see her. They were in a still position, very rarely moving a muscle and apologising to each other when they did. Her right foot had lost a shoe and when she moved her toes she could not locate it, no doubt flung around the carriage and long gone. She still had no feeling in her left foot. It became clearer as the tiniest amount of light appeared that the crash was worse than she had ever imagined. At no point did she realise that there was a brick wall at the end of the tunnel. She was aware then that what she had been resting her left hand on all this time wasn't an arm rest, it was a body. She had a long wait still as the firemen had to recover everything around her first in order to free her from the twisted wreckage of train parts, bodies and other survivors who could be freed quicker. As one body was removed in front of her, she saw the dress had been torn away revealing a brown petticoat. Recalling this image years later she would say, "I have a vivid memory of thinking how I would not want to be rescued wearing a brown petticoat!"

Marian King came round again and found that she was face to face with a fireman. There was now a lot of motion around her, people talking to her in order to make sure she kept awake and was aware of what was going on around her. She realised that her legs were caught up in a chair underneath her, part of it being upwards at an angle and it had ended up in between her legs, luckily not breaking any bones. Only at that point did she realise she wasn't on the floor anymore, she must have been flung up by the collision and landed on top of a huge pile of debris. After what seemed a lifetime the firemen removed the seat from under her.

Looking around her, she saw a man next to her who she wasn't even aware was there until now, he had dislocated his shoulder and was being seen to by another fireman before they would remove him. Firemen were asking those left alive if they need morphine for the pain. Even if you said no they gave you a dose anyway as it was most likely shock that was keeping the pain away and it would hit them at a later stage if that was the case. Being more awake now she could hear talking and people crying out for help, "Help me God!"

Suddenly the man behind her starting rocking about and then she realised that he had been across her right leg all this time. She felt her ligament suddenly tear and although it was a horrible feeling, the pain didn't come due to the morphine given to her, but she still felt the sensation of it. The firemen were trying their hardest to not cause any more suffering as they manoeuvred chairs and metal fragments about to clear the space. The man next to her was now ready to be pulled out, slowly moving him out through what looked like a hole in the roof of the carriage. As he was being lifted upwards, a part of his shoe was being dragged up her leg and was causing her some discomfort.

"Oh it's scratching me," she said, to which one of the firemen suddenly erupted in anger.

"Scratching!! That's nothing compared to what I've just seen!"

Feeling bad she said, "Oh...I'm sorry."

"No," he said, "I'm sorry," and he continued, with the realisation that soon she would be out and away.

Looking down she saw the woman whom she had seen getting on at Old Street with her hair tied up very tightly. She was dead.

"Do you like dancing?" said a stranger. This was fireman Brian Goodfellow who was now shining his torch on her. (It seems like the dancing line worked every time in getting people to think outside of the situation.)

"Erm…oh yes!" she said, like the others she was wondering why he was asking such a strange question.

"Well, when you get out of here I will take you dancing," he said.

It was only later on that she realised that random talking like this would not only keep them awake but it would keep her spirits up and take her mind of what was going on around her.

Several hours had now gone by since the crash and a voice behind her said he needed to go to the loo. "For Christ sake just go," said another voice. Nobody could move so there was nothing they could do for each other. She had now lost feeling in her legs; being under a lot of pressure they had started to swell a fair bit.

After a very long wait trapped in the carriage, it was at last safe for her to be moved. A stretcher was lowered next to her and they manoeuvred her onto it, strapping her tightly with her arms crossed. She then was hoisted up out through the hole in the roof before being turned on her back with an oxygen mask strapped to her face. She was then turned back on her side and sent down the side of the train in between the carriage and the tunnel wall. There was always somebody holding on to each end with one of them saying, "Don't worry, we'll get you through."

The images of the dead were flashing by her as she was making the short but difficult journey out of the tunnel. Because of the morphine dose these images were not registering in her mind as being real, this had most likely saved her from what could have been a heavy amount of mental trauma. But at long last the lights of the platform greeted her. She realised then she was covered in soot but she was alive, breathing and on her way to safety. A saline drip was administered in her arm and the nurse began talking to her as she made her way up to street level to the ambulance. At this point Marian asked what time it was. The nurse replied, "It is nearly lunchtime," and she thought, oh I got on at nearly 9 o'clock, realising she had been stuck in the train for around three to four hours now. She was placed in the ambulance with the nurse and sent on her way.

In a lot of cases, due to the soot covering their faces, marks had to be made on the survivors being dragged out with felt tip pens to highlight injuries such as fractures. The severity of their injuries was categorised by marking one to three crosses on their forehead. The noise of the rescue operation made some examinations difficult and the patients had to be removed from the site to be able to be rushed to hospital in the hope of being saved. Listening for a heartbeat was impossible. Another problem for the rescuers was the lighting, which was very low-powered due to the track current being off; emergency lighting would have to be rigged.

*

Throughout the morning news was filtering to TVs and radios around the country and very soon the first newspapers would be screaming headlines on the disaster.

At around midday, at Silvertown fire station, the teleprinters rang out to say that the team would now be dispatched to attend the scene at Moorgate. By now the disaster was on a huge scale and they would need every bit of help they could get. There were still people trapped in the wreckage and the death toll was thought to be numbered in the dozens already. The messages said that so many pumps were required that due to the extreme heat in the tunnel the men had to be relieved at regular intervals. There were only two engines at this station so they sent one out with a crew of four and left the second one on standby in case of other emergencies. Norman Paulding took the outbound engine over to the scene and the twenty minute drive to the city ended with it parked up near to the station on Moorgate itself. The team then disembarked and made their way over to the control unit vehicle where they would be designated jobs for them to do, which in this case was to head straight to the platform.

When they got down there it seemed a bit dark, with a lot of people doing their jobs and relieving each other. The heat was really starting to build up now and after several hours of being kitted up in full fire-fighting gear a lot of the rescuers just needed some cold air from outside. Taking over from one of the crews, Paulding's men entered through the back of carriage three and out into the tunnel side to get to the front. A scaling ladder had been rigged and that allowed them to enter part of the train where the roof had come away. It took ten minutes of struggling to get from the platform down to carriage one with no breathing apparatus.

At this point the only two people left alive in the wreckage were WPC

Margaret Liles and Jeff Benton; everybody else around them was dead. Reaching the two survivors Norman put some water on Jeff's lips to stop them drying out.

"I'll never get out of here," he said sadly

"Yes you will," said Norman, reassuring them both that it was only a matter of time before they would be freed. Looking now at the scene in carriage one, he could see that part of the chassis of the coach had come up between their legs and it was that which was trapping them. Cold cutting had already been tried and that hadn't worked, hot cutting was out of the question, not only because of the heat but it would take all the oxygen that they had in this little area. Not only that, there was a possible risk of fire if they did.

Climbing under the train, the team saw that where the two survivors were could be reached from below the carriage and there was a trapdoor under each carriage, which was handy at this point. It took a while to crawl over to this trapdoor but it showed that you could just about reach Margaret's foot if nothing else.

It now became clear that the only way to free both survivors was to amputate her foot there in the tunnel. Surgeons began discussing how they would operate in such bad conditions, but it was not an impossibility and they could get the tools over to do it. They were taken into the tunnel with their equipment and shown the scene. There was no other way for it. Bodies now had to be shifted to make room for the operation and when the time was right they told Margaret and Jeff what was about to happen.

The surgeon was working hard in the tunnel and was getting worn out in the heat. In the end he was told to get out, if he had any kind of injury, even just a small scratch, from handling a dead body, he would get blood poisoning, this being a man who was wearing a tunic instead of the firefighters' heavy, durable rescue gear. He made his way back onto the platform to see the nurses and he was given some oxygen to help him recover and get his breath back.

"How do you feel?" said one nurse.

"Yeah...I...feel alright," he said

"Glass of water?" she offered.

"I'd sooner have a beer," he said sarcastically.

He soon recovered himself and went topside for a while. By now Norman Paulding's team had been down there long enough and it was time to leave and let the relief teams take over. As the day wore on it became apparent that the fire-fighters were having to be relieved every fifteen to twenty minutes in order for them to perform to a workable standard. The heat was now going up to around 100 degrees Fahrenheit and threatened to go higher.

*

Police Constable Alan Francis was on annual holiday when he heard the first news reports on LBC radio. *"Reports are coming in of a train crash at Moorgate station, there are casualties. As news comes in we will report developments."* As the crash was on Wood Street's division he rang the station straight away to discover his deputy, Superintendent Smith, was already at the scene. He rang the control room to ask if he was required but at the time there was not enough information and he was told that he wasn't needed.

He went out and didn't ring them again until the afternoon when the BBC was reporting that the incident had become a serious one. He made his way to the scene to speak to Brian Fisher who was there with the Mivvi Van, positioned next to the Fire Brigade and Ambulance Control vans, all being in close communication with each other. Looking around, Alan realised that Brian Fisher's master planning and ability had come together like clockwork. A situation, he saw, that was both well handled and professional.

It now became apparent that there were a large number of dead bodies that needed to be recovered. While the teams at the front were working on the last two survivors, the rest of the crews became aware that there was nobody else left alive. One of the firemen to help move the victims was 26-year-old Paul Efreme, who had only been in the fire service for two years. Based in Shoreditch, he had been on a breathing apparatus course that day and had come over to Moorgate in the evening. He was a very junior fireman and he wanted to see what was going on and see if he could help. As he was still doing the course he technically shouldn't have been there, but here he was voluntarily going into the tunnel to give assistance to retrieve the bodies. As the front of the train was a mass of twisted metal and very dangerous, they wouldn't let him go right to the front, he would instead carry out what the other teams recovered and take them out of the wreckage.

The bodies were placed in coffins and laid out to be identified a few blocks away. Francis McPherson was a mounted police officer who had been riding along Cheapside when he got the call at 0915 that morning to return to the stables and head to the mortuary. Now it was up to him to identify the Moorgate crash victims and speak to the families direct; when he was satisfied that he had all the information he needed he would lead them to a small chapel to officially identify them. After a positive ID he would then hand over any clothes and possessions they had, noting in a pocket book what was taken and by whom, having that countersigned by a WPC working next to him. This was very sad and upsetting for him, time and time again seeing bereaved relatives coming to identify a son, a daughter, a wife, a husband. Each time leaving in tears, each time having nothing left of their life except a small bag of worthless trinkets and personal effects, most of which were damaged, dirty or blood-stained.

The WRVS made regular contact with them and supplied them with food and hot drinks, whereas the nearby BP offices had called in all available staff and supplied them with dinners all night. Francis would stay at his post for twenty-nine hours, not leaving until 11.30 on the Saturday morning.

*

Almost every day Tozammel Syed would ring his wife Shameen up at work to see how she was. Normally he would do this once he had got to his office and sorted himself out for the day's work. At 9.30 he picked up the phone and dialled her number. There was no reply, but it then dawned on him that she had been told that her mother in Bangladesh had sent her something to a friend's address in London and that she had previously mentioned about picking it up. Maybe that's where she is, he thought, placing down the receiver; he would try again later. When he did ring back a colleague picked up the phone. No she was not at work yet, probably still coming back from picking up the parcel, although now it was unusually late for her. It was at 11.30 that the bank rang him directly to say that she had still not turned up for work and that news was filtering out onto the streets that there had been a train crash at Moorgate station. She was always very punctual and they thought they had better tell him with it being so strange that she hadn't turned up. After that phone call he got one not much later, it was Shameen's brother Farhad who was living with them. He was a student at the time and was still at home; he had heard about the crash and told Tozammel that it might be a good idea if he came home to await any news. Tozammel spoke to his boss and he agreed that it was a good idea if he went home, but, instead of heading home, he went straight to Moorgate station where he noticed that Farhad was already there. They asked around if anyone had seen Shameen, but none of the usual commuters could help them and they didn't want to ask the rescue services as they all looked really busy. Heading to Pubali Bank they saw their friend from the flat above, Sailla, who confirmed that she had still not turned up for work. Ringing around friends and relatives it became clear that the searching was in vain. For these two men wandering around, panic now started to set in.

*

While rescue work was continuing, the emergency crews allowed one journalist and a photographer down to see what was going on, but on the condition that they made the information available to the other journalists. Gerard Kemp from the Daily Telegraph was that journalist. What he saw was printed in every newspaper as rescuers battled their way forward.

By mid morning a breakdown train had managed to manoeuvre itself within winching distance of the train and started to tow away the rear three cars at a rate of one inch every ten minutes. Normal passenger services were still being carried on, with trains being stopped at Old Street to let passengers disembark before the empty the train was sent onwards to platform 10 to reverse back up the line.

At this same time there were still a number of people trapped in carriage one, a group of survivors who were struggling in the darkness: Jill Dunderdale, twenty-two, and her boyfriend, 23-year-old Jonathan Ludbrook who had sat next to each other; 42-year-old Audrey Beard from Highbury; and Marian King.

While Marian was trapped in the wreckage of the train, all kinds of people were coming to her mum's shop saying "have you heard the news?" She would say "no I haven't what's happened?" and then she was told that there had been a tube crash. The mother of a young woman named Jane Simpson heard that her daughter had got on the train and she was very distressed. They were pretty close and both families knew each other. As she was sympathising with her she realised that Marian was on that train too. Marian's mother immediately rang her work and soon they all realised that she had never arrived that morning. On a Friday it was tradition that your work friends would bring coffee to your desk and when you got in you would have a nice fresh coffee waiting for you when you got in. Marian's coffee was still on her desk. They put her on hold as they wanted Mr Johnson the manager to talk to her instead. His opening words to her mum were, "Marian isn't here…just yet…she is probably somewhere having a coffee," at which she immediately realised that not only was he as clueless as everybody else over her whereabouts, Marian also wouldn't do something like that as it was out of character. Her dad now took over the conversation and although Marian's boss was trying to be tactful, the truth was immediate. If something like this had gone on close by then she would have found a phone box straight away and rung home.

    They started listening out on the news for the emergency number and once they had it they reported her as a missing person whom they suspected had got on that train. They took her name and said they would be in touch with any news. They heard nothing until 3pm that afternoon after they had got her 17-year-old brother Robert to come home early from Enfield School. He wasn't happy at first as it was football that afternoon, something he enjoyed, although he soon realised that there was something seriously wrong. When somebody from the helpline phoned at 3pm they couldn't say whether she was dead or alive, all they could say was that they had heard her name mentioned at London Hospital. After hanging up the family travelled down to the hospital wondering what was going to greet them. Was she alive or was she laid out ready to be identified? The worry was as intense as it could possibly be.

    In actual fact Marian was doing well. She had arrived at the hospital and met a doctor whom she thought looked remarkably like actor Oliver Reed. They proceeded to cut off her clothes and jacket, an act about which she was gutted as she had made the jacket herself. The doctor started examining her leg and feeling for pulses, as it was still numb and she couldn't feel much. If she had torn ligaments then she would need a plaster on it that was for sure. She gave a moan to him saying "Oh I don't feel right," to which he slapped the leg and said in a joke fashion "I've seen worse than you. You're gonna be OK." The doctor was pleased that he had seen somebody who was sure to recover, he had seen much worse in the hours that he had been there that morning. Thankful that the doctor had reassured her, she began to feel a little more relaxed.

    As she was wheeled out of the examination room through the double doors, she came face to face with her waiting family sat on a row of chairs.

They had all been openly crying, not knowing what was going on with her. As she was wheeled past she just said "Hello!" at which her brother leapt up and threw off her covers, making sure she was all in one piece with all her limbs. It was one thing to survive Moorgate, but quite another to survive in one piece, especially in carriage one! She was so pleased to see them she said that it was like meeting them all for the first time. Every one of them was still in shock at the events of the day, so much so that her mother came down with a cold very soon after with the stress of it all. The doctors left her on the trolley for a few minutes to talk to her family. Everything still seemed like a dream, she only remembered bits of what went on so that meant she had lost consciousness several times. She couldn't move much by now and had no control over her upper limbs, having to wait a while to get feeling back eventually. According to her dad, when he looked at her bruised back, it looked like "blackcurrant jam" it was that battered, although thankfully there were no broken bones.

*

In the nearby police incident room, one officer had a colour coding system for the victims. They had to use cards with names on to link with the property recovered or person on file, each one having a different colour – dead (red), seriously injured (stripy pink), minor injuries (plain pink) and missing (white). He would receive many phone calls from people who had friends missing that day, work colleagues who were not turning up, neighbours' and family details continuously being passed down the line and logged.

The room held a white card for a 17-year-old girl who had left home on the morning of the crash and hadn't been seen or heard from all weekend. Seventeen frantic phone calls were met with no news on her whereabouts. With several bodies still trapped in the wreckage and the parents now convinced that their daughter had been killed, the girl simply returned home oblivious of what had been going on. When she walked through the door her mother fainted.

After the identification would come the post mortems; each body had to be examined by Professor Keith Simpson and then released to the families for burial. Some of them would be requested to be flown to their home countries immediately. Most would stay in the UK where they had lived.

The identifications officer would later tell the author of the incredible daily battle with the heat down on the platform. "Of course it was mighty hot in the train station and one clear memory I have is the Army fetching up a mobile water heater powered by coal and wood which had last been used by Montgomery's troops (8th and 3rd Army) in Africa during the battle with Rommel. It was used on this occasion to provide hot showers for the firemen; it being installed in a large green canvas tent. It was operated by REME personnel I think and chugged away happily – not bad considering we moved on from Africa to the toe of Italy for the last huge drive north in about late 1943/early1944. The machine must have been around forty-five to fifty years old at least. It did the trick though."

In the afternoon, police photographer Tony Wallis was able to get into the tunnel to continue his job. Now that most of the survivors had been released he could snap away at the scene, staying clear of the current rescue operation on Margaret and Jeff at the front. Walking down the side of the train he noticed there were people dead just sitting there as if nothing had happened. He knew Margaret was trapped up front, he felt sorry for her as he knew her from work and realised she had only just passed her training. As he was taking photos from every angle the firemen were bringing out items that ranged from handbags and shoes to a pot plant and overnight bags. Numbers were placed on the bodies and more photos were taken from different angles. Tony would stay long into the night before being relieved by another police photographer named Pete Simmonds.

Tony would have to sign in and out at a desk so he didn't stay in the station for longer than was necessary or end up getting stuck down there. Whenever a body was recovered he was called onto the platform to photograph it; there were only a few of them in the department so they were very busy at this point. Tony would also take the photos as the autopsies were being carried out later. For him he would be working long into the week as the evidence was collected and the train dismantled. Another member of the photographic team was acting sergeant Pete James who would be working over at the mortuary stripping the victims down and putting their possessions together for relatives to use for identification purposes.

*

Bob Ainsworth worked for the Continental Bank of Chicago in Moorgate and used to come to work on the Northern Line. One of his work colleagues had not shown up for work that day and hearing about the crash made him worried that he had been caught up in it. They put it down initially as him taking a day off sick, the news about Moorgate coming in that it had only been a shunt. As the extent of the disaster became apparent it was clear that his colleague had been amongst those killed. He had had to work a little later than usual today so didn't leave work until around 6-7pm, with Moorgate station still open at the side entrance for the other lines. As he approached the entrance of the station, he noticed a large van and in it were stacked coffins. There were a couple of police officers and only four other men with them. Bob and a few passers-by lent a hand to get the coffins into a room with a black curtain across it, ready for the victims to be placed into them from the platform. After he had helped with several of these coffins, the room now full with about twenty of them in there, he headed off to resume his original journey home. Giving a few minutes of his time that day helped the police officers in a grim job, but it was one that would stay with Bob for the rest of his life.

At around the same time, about 6pm, the Silverton fire crew returned back to their station after being relieved by their own second appliance that they had kept back that morning. Norman Paulding left the scene wondering what would happen to the two trapped passengers and how long they would have to be down there. While at the fire station he changed out of his kit, had a wash and went home.

For Frank David, he came off duty very late and went back to his HQ first. He remarked that he looked like a chimney sweep as he got himself showered and ready to go home. He was pleased that the equipment used in the tunnel had worked so well.

*

Barry Coppock still had no idea how much of an escape he had just gone through that morning. At work he told his colleagues about what had happened, but as word spread about the seriousness of the crash, it soon became apparent that Barry had literally walked away from a disaster. Over lunchtime he had walked over to see the station, which by now was closed off from Ropemakers Street to London Wall. There was no immediate information as to how bad it was, but looking at the number of appliances that had showed up it was obviously worse than he thought.

As he left work that evening at 5.30pm he was shaking as he realised how lucky he had been. What shocked him more was the fact he had just had so little realisation of the seriousness and thought it was just an over-run of the platform, not thinking for a minute that the train had hit a brick wall and killed many of people. He headed home as normal from Liverpool Street station and picked up a copy of the Evening Standard from a guy who sold it at the top of Eldham Street (nowadays it is at the new entrance to Liverpool Street station). He would always be there from lunchtime onwards selling papers. Looking down at the headlines he read the first reports saying that there were people trapped in the wreckage still. All he could think about was how he had chosen the right carriage; it could so easily have been him that they were now trying to get out alive. Or worse.

Douglas Thomson was also having a bad time realising he was a survivor of a major disaster. He started to cry uncontrollably when he spoke to a work colleague about it, so she took him for another coffee and a brandy. He was sent home at lunchtime as he was in no fit state to work and looked dreadful, a colleague walking him to Finsbury Square where the bus took him back home.

London Underground worker Dave Bolton had been to the scene after hearing the news, he had to be at Tower Hill anyway for 1330 to start work. He saw the ticket collector in tears as people were bringing up survivors. One of the cake shops was sending food to the firemen, the place was crowded with people all with a job to do. With the heat being unbearable and with no job to do there, he went on his way.

Tim Hatton spent all day crawling through the wreckage, but his wife hadn't even heard about it. Needless to say she was shocked when he returned home that night.

At 6pm police officer Brian Tibbenham was on the national news bulletin giving the details to the cameras about what had taken place below their feet. He would stay on scene for another two hours before handing his duty over to another inspector and heading home, but not before having a look below ground to see what the situation was now that most of the survivors were out and away.

*

The police photography teams were there all day and well into the night, recording everything and anything that may be useful to the investigation.

Bodies had to be photographed where they lay, interesting objects that were recovered, dial positions, pipe work, cables and personal possessions. The investigators would later tell the teams which photographs they required for their job and which they didn't. Adrian Eatwell, Tony Wallis and Andy Day had all been on scene throughout the day and had continued long into the night.

For Chris Robertson, he had gone to work at a civil engineering company at 0930 that morning in Westminster and was unaware anything had gone on in the middle of the city until around lunchtime. Thinking that his fiancée Marian King may have been on board, he tried to ring her at work but for some reason couldn't get through. It was unusual for nobody to answer the phones but still there was most likely nothing to worry about.

It wasn't until 1830 when he phoned her home that he spoke to her mother. Marian had been in the crash and was in hospital. It came as a huge shock but at least he was spared all the worry during the day when there was nothing he could have done. He spoke on the phone to her brother and he said that he had come back from the hospital not long ago and gave him an update on his sister. He didn't go to the family home as he didn't want to feel like he was intruding, but at least he knew now she was safe.

For Ambulanceman Dave Tovey, he was almost finished for the day, taking one member of staff home to the south east of London. This man had been treated after fainting as he had come face to face with the van unloading coffins. By the time his jobs were done, Dave was told to sign off and go home.

*

Now it was late into the night and the problem was still how to get the two remaining survivors out of the wreckage safely. Margaret and Jeff were now in grave danger after being down there since the crash had happened at 0846 that morning, with no food and drink save for what the firemen could wet their lips with.

By now it was obvious that after several hours of moving around and pulling and tugging, the only way to free them both was to cut off Margaret's foot at the ankle. She remarked to the fireman that she thought she had broken her ankle as she could no longer feel it and hadn't done for hours. He just replied that yes, that might be the case. Although the workers changed shifts very quickly it made no difference to either of them; she started feeling that her time was up and that she should be just left there and go in peace. She was soon pulled back to her senses and reassured that nobody was going anywhere while ever she was trapped down there.

The next stage was to prepare her for the operation. After telling her that the firemen were fighting over who was going to carry her out, they said they were going to put her to sleep to get her out. "This seemed an excellent idea by that stage!" she said later. An injection into her hand and she waited. She then panicked as she realised she was not asleep and said that she was still awake! No sooner had she said that and she passed out as the drugs kicked in.

With a PC Venning holding a torch, the surgeon got to work on her foot. This was going to be not only a very delicate operation but also it had to be done quickly, this wasn't a hospital it was a wrecked train covered in soot and bodies, this entire situation ran the risk of major blood loss or infection. They had to release her and get her out of the train as quickly as possible. Unfortunately for Jeff he had to watch the entire episode play out in front of him. They couldn't sedate him in case they accidentally started cutting him and they would need to know about it or they would have two major injuries to contend with.

Sawing away at her lower leg, within a short while she was freed and wrapped up, heading to the platform as quickly as possible. She was ushered up the stairs and taken out of the station to a glare of photographers' flashlights. The ambulance doors slammed shut and she was whisked at full speed over to St Bart's Hospital. Now Margaret was freed and on her way, there was one more person to recover. This was now considered the easy part as it was Margaret that had been trapping Jeff and stopping him from getting out.

With badly injured legs, Jeff Benton was hauled out of carriage one with relative ease and taken the same way to the platform before heading up to street level. After thirteen hours, the rescue operation was now officially over. The next stage of the operation was recovery of the victims. This would take considerably longer.

*

For Jeff's family the day had brought both shock and uncertainty. His wife Valerie Benton took a phone call just before 9am from his father asking if he had left for work that morning as there were some problems with trains going into Moorgate station and he had not shown up for work yet. She confirmed that he had left as usual, at which point he suggested that she take a taxi across from her work place in Marble Arch to the City. She was not aware of anything happening yet, news was only just filtering through at that point, but when she hailed a taxi she was told in a strong cockney accent, "I'm not sure if I can get you there lady, there's some kind of problem with the tube station at Moorgate and traffic is being diverted, real bad it is." She explained that her husband was due to be on a Drayton Park train to Moorgate yet had not arrived at work. Realising that this was an emergency, he sped across London and she arrived at Wedd Durlacher's offices to find both Jeff's father and boss waiting for her. Val takes up the story from here…

"The update was, that there had been some kind of accident with the train into Moorgate station, but passengers from the train were slowly arriving at work, somewhat shaken and covered in soot. Some of the passengers had sustained injuries and these people were taken to St Bartholomew's Hospital in the City. At this stage, still no news of Jeff, so we went to St Bartholomew's and were advised they did not have Jeff on their casualty list and they were not taking further patients as their A & E section was now full. All further casualties were being taken to the London Hospital in Whitechapel, our next stop and where I was to spend the next ten hours.

All the while Mr Stevens was checking in with his office and other hospitals to see if Jeff had been taken elsewhere. Mr Benton remained with me throughout the day.

It was around 2.30pm that I became aware of the severity of the situation. On the table in the waiting room, someone had left the midday newspaper and the front page headlines were 'Moorgate Tube Train Horror Crash... At least 30 dead and many injured.' This was when I started to be concerned that he may be injured, but never did I think he was dead. The day progressed and although we were being updated there was still no news of Jeff. Many people came and went from the waiting area as they received news of their family or friends. Small talk was minimal, we all just waited and prayed that our loved ones would be safe."

In the meantime Jeff's brother Keith didn't even know anything was going on until somebody at work that morning said, "There's been a really bad train crash in London." Like many other people, they would have no reason to think it would affect them or their family. In the evening there was a staff volleyball match with drinks in the pub after. He rang his wife up who immediately said that Jeff had been in the train crash. When they contacted the emergency number they couldn't say if he was alive, dead or even if he was on the train.

By 6pm that evening, his father decided he should go home to be with his wife and children as he felt his support was needed there. Val wandered around the waiting area and the gardens of the hospital. At around 9.30 that night word was out that two people were trapped in the front carriage, a man and a woman and it was difficult to get to them. The names were released which confirmed that it was Jeff who was trapped; further confirmation came when she heard he had said that he "could do with a nice cold beer", him being a fan of the real ales.

By now Keith had returned home and put the news on at 10pm to see a live report from Kate Adie just as the final survivor was being brought out. Live on their front room TV was Jeff on a stretcher giving a smile to the cameras as he was brought into fresh air. "Bloody hell there he is!" shouted Keith, absolutely elated to see him safely brought out. Val had nothing more to do that night and was sent home to rest, exhausted but happy that Jeff was alive.

Meanwhile in St Bart's, Margaret Liles was waking up as she was waiting with a young nurse to go up in a lift. Margaret asked her what had happened, and she was told that her foot had been amputated in order to free her. She calmly said that she was lucky to be alive before drifting off back to sleep again.

5. Searching for the missing

For most of the survivors, their horror in the tunnel had ended, at least physically. Several more would have to have their injuries tended to for years to come. It was the unseen injuries that would cause the biggest problems, the trauma of what they had seen and heard would haunt them for months and years; in a lot of cases such images never fade. But it was families of those who were missing in the tunnel whose pain was only just being realised. At the site of the crash a Red Cross volunteer was comforting a woman who had lost her husband, she heard her break down and say, "It was his birthday! My children and I were waiting for him to come home to give him his presents. He was thirty-five today."

When the family of Stephen Payne heard of a major rail disaster in the City of London they didn't even connect it with him, let alone begin to get worried. He had gone to work as usual and always took the above ground national rail trains to Liverpool Street. But little did they know that a friend of Stephen's mother, Sheila, had told him that getting the tube to Moorgate would be a lot quicker. Today he had been late for work and remembered the conversation, so in order for him to arrive on time he decided, just this once, to take this advice.

It was later in the day that his girlfriend Marion rang Stephen's parents asking if they had seen him. No of course they hadn't, he was at work. She then explained that he hadn't arrived at work that morning. It was three phone calls to his office later and Marion still had no answer. Then the bank rang, Sheila answering the phone, only to be told that there had been an accident at Moorgate station that morning. It was then that they realised he had to have been somehow involved. This was the only explanation as to where he could be.

Not far away from the Payne household, at around 10.30am, an elderly neighbour saw Fred Donovan in the front garden and called out to him. "Have you heard? There's been a big crash!" he said. Although it was bad to hear they both thought no more about it. He must have heard the first reports over the radio as news filtered through. Fred was self-employed and today he had decided to take a day off. It wasn't until midday that he was suddenly approached by a police officer.

"Mr Donovan?"

"Yes."

"Your daughter Janet, Mr Donovan?"
"No Janice."
"I've got some bad news.... Your daughter has been killed in the accident."
Fred stood there shocked.
"Where's your wife?" asked the officer.
"She's at work," replied Fred.
"Shall I tell her at work?"
"No…get her from work," he said.

In the meantime, Joan was at her work at Thornes Electrical doing her usual task of hand soldering on electric boards. It was a happy day so far as one of her work friends was leaving and getting married and so they were singing silly songs about weddings, much to the enjoyment of them all. At around 12.30 she saw the police officer enter her work. She was due to finish anyway at 1pm but seeing him approach she automatically thought it was her son who had been involved in an accident, maybe he had fallen off a roof? She was escorted away by the police, but they didn't tell her what had happened, they just asked if there was anybody who could come with her, which her friend Jean was only too obliged to do. It was when she returned home that the awful truth became apparent. That early on in the day, Janice must have been one of the first victims to be recovered out of the wreckage. By around 4pm Fred had the heartbreaking task of going to go and identify the body, Jean's husband driving him down. By now they had cleaned the soot off her and they were told she had died in hospital. Her death certificate simply said for cause of death – "Lacerated brain". While he was out performing this sad duty, a WPC sat with Joan at home. Janice's fiancé Roger wasn't allowed to view the body as he was not officially next of kin. Fred picked up her few belongings – clothes, a handbag and one solitary shoe – and brought them home, burying them in the back garden. She had been identified by the provisional driving licence in her purse, which contained nothing but a few coins. For them it was over, for others it could be several days before news came through of their loved ones.

*

For the family of 17-year-old David Wilson, they were going about their business like on any other Friday. His family take up the story of what happened next: *"We all made our individual ways to work or continued with our Friday routine be it in Islington, Maidenhead, Holland Park, or Enfield, the normality only interrupted by the overhearing of a radio news report of an incident at Moorgate Station which did not immediately ring alarm bells, although a little concern perhaps was registering among us. Our eldest sibling Brenda was the first of us to be made aware of the possible nature of the tragedy, she having been telephoned from Islington. A young lady neighbour travelled the same journey at around the same time as David and she had raised concerns with mum. She immediately knew that there was good reason to be fearful for David."*

Telephone calls with his college confirmed the fear that David had not completed his journey, so from that moment on the whole family mustered to their home at Hume Court as quickly as they could. Aided by the efforts of a family member who was then in the Met Police, they established a link with London Transport at 55 Broadway, but such information that was provided was non-committal and vague; the BBC Television news reports were, in truth, the only real source of information they had. *"As the horror of it all unfolded on TV we knew that our David was now listed among the missing passengers."*

At around lunchtime Janet King noticed one of the first news boards that had been put out for the early editions of the London newspaper, The Evening Standard, announcing that there had been deaths in a crash at Moorgate. This was the first she had heard of anything, so she immediately rang her fiancé Peter Bradbury's work. They told her that they hadn't heard from him today, leading to a feeling of pure dread enveloping her entire body. She would spend the rest of the day and long into the night calling the hospitals, sitting and waiting, hoping that he was alright and that it was all a bit of a misunderstanding. Hoping that if he *was* involved, he was alive. As the hours ticked by ever slower, that thought was slowly diminishing.

For Lesley Hall, she had heard about the crash and immediately went down to the scene to give blood. When she arrived there was already a huge number of people queuing up so she decided against it, she would be hanging around for a long time, if she actually got seen at all. She had no idea that her family was about to be involved in this in another, more tragic way. At the West End of London, her sisters Frances and Christine Hall, who both worked together at the same place, heard people talking about a radio report of this terrible event that was unfolding in their capital. Again, nobody connected their own family with it and wouldn't do for a long time to come.

It was around 6pm that evening that their sister Joy was settling down with a meal and saw the news reports of the crash, followed minutes later by Terry's boyfriend ringing her asking if she had been seen, as she was supposed to be with him and hadn't come home that night. "Have you two had a row?" she said, still unable to process the jigsaw of information that was slowly creeping through. By now the family were starting to look at the images being broadcast on their TV and have a sickening gut feeling that there may be a connection. Hopefully they were wrong.

That evening, their parents got into the car and went down to Moorgate to see if they could get some information. They couldn't get close to the disaster site so they parked up in Finsbury Square. Walking around the area they got as close as they could to the scene without getting in the way, noticing the amount of ambulances lined up. It was here they saw an old friend, George Flynn, who happened to be an ambulance driver. He said that he couldn't access the crash site itself so the ambulance crews had just as much information as the Hall family did, his job was just to wait at the station entrance for any casualties to appear and deal with them as they came out. This was now becoming agony for the Halls, they had no information on Terry other than the fact that she was missing. Everything pointed to her being on that train, but like everybody else they hoped it was all a mistake and she would be there waiting when they got back home. When they returned back home they were met by the rest of the family, hungry for news, but with none to receive.

The mother of BP worker Alistair Gordon was also starting to become anxious – normally if something happened in the middle of London he would ring home to reassure her that he was OK and not caught up in anything. At around 5pm that evening she got a phone call from his boss to say that he had not shown up for work that morning. The police were called and his home was broken into where they found no trace of him. A search of hospitals by the family revealed that they had nobody by that name. It would be Sunday 2nd March, a whole forty-eight hours after the crash, when they would get confirmation that his body was in the tunnel at Moorgate, news that devastated his 70-year-old mother. She had already lost Alistair's brother Ian in 1964 after he had emigrated to Canada and had died there not long after. She never got over the loss of her two sons but the whole time she kept her grief to herself and died just eleven years later after developing what appeared to be the onset of dementia.

*

Fred Wonderling Jr. was a nightshift worker at Smithfield meat market in the city and had come home at around 0830 that Friday morning. Instead of sleeping all day he was going to take his mother-in-law to Whittington Hospital for an appointment, which was in itself no drama. But it was on the way back from there that they saw the first news stands announcing a train crash at Moorgate station. Fred turned to his wife Carol: "I'm sure that's the train dad gets," he said.

They arrived back at home after dropping Carol's mother off and put the TV on for the news. Immediately they were met by coverage of the crash, which was concerning, but he didn't want to worry his father's wife, May, by ringing her up and telling her when there was no reason to, at least not just yet. Being tired from his nightshift at the market and after driving to the hospital, he went to bed for the afternoon at long last.

When he woke up in the evening he again saw the news and decided to make sure that his dad was alright, by now he should be home from work so he would get confirmation that he was safe. He walked out of his flat, down the road to the phone box and dialled his number. The person who answered was not his father or his stepmother, it was a police officer. He was told immediately that in fact his father *had* been on the train and that tragically he had been killed in the crash. Shocked, Fred was unprepared for such sudden and heartbreaking news. To make it worse the officer said to him that they needed somebody to identify his body. "Your mother is in too much of a state," he said, referring to May.

With all kinds of thoughts going round his head he went to Wood Street Police Station front desk, where he was directed to Moor Lane just up the road, where a temporary mortuary had been set up. He made his way round to the door and the officer standing there directed him where to go. Inside were metal lockers and boxes leaning about all over the place, and he now had to wait to be called in. Very soon he was ushered into a room; he saw more of these containers were there. At around 7pm that Friday night, preparing himself for the worst, Fred gave the nod. A lid was pulled back and there was his father's face, peaceful and at rest as if he was asleep, the only visible sign on him being a mark on his head. Satisfied that it was definitely his father Fred Snr., he walked away. An officer gave him a small black plastic bag containing his father's belongings. As he handed them over he said to him, "Let me give you a bit of advice...don't look in the bag. If you can burn it, burn it."

He never looked in the bag but he did throw it in the bin as soon as he could. Who knows what was in there and what it was covered in. He would be better off not knowing. Carol had seen one of the firemen nearby and asked him what it was like down in the tunnel. He described the scene of carnage below as being like opening "all the pages of a book and then slamming them all together."

Of all his possessions, Fred chose to keep his father's watch. (Due to father and son having the same name this created a lot of confusion for people. Many locals thought it was Fred Jr. that had been killed and in 2004 he received a letter from a woman who had been in primary school with him as a child. She remarked how she thought he had been killed in the crash and how pleased she was that he was still alive.)

*

For the family of the train driver Leslie Newson, their journey of grief was going to be a lot different from anybody else's. His wife Helen was at home when she had been told by a police officer; they immediately knocked on the neighbour's downstairs to come up to comfort her. Their daughter then rang Sandra Newson to say there had been a crash. At 11am Helen rang her to fill her in on what few details were filtering through. "What hospital is he in?" she said. "I will come and collect you and bring you home," which she did. By then the news was out that this was a major incident and Les Newson was at the heart of the story; people began knocking on the doors every hour which would then go on for days at a time, in many cases for years more to come.

Police turned up at Diane's work to take her back to her parents' flat where the family would stay and wait for news. An official from London Transport came to see Helen and told her not to talk to the press. Although her husband was also a member of the union, nobody from there came to see her. The only comfort outside of the immediate family came from Les's friend, John Simmons, but it seemed like he was very trusting of London Transport. But then again so would Les have been if it was the other way round. Now it was just a wait and see situation. Wait for news, see what would happen. Never would they feel more helpless.

*

Leslie Cook was working at Tottenham that day in a factory when there was talk amongst his colleagues about a tube crash. He turned around and said, "Christ Almighty! Where?" and rushed to phone home. He got no reply, but then again he wouldn't have, his wife was at work and so was his daughter Janet. But when he got home that evening a friend and his wife came over to tell him that their son was on the train…and so was Janet. Their lad had come away with facial injuries, but there was no word on Janet. With confirmation that their daughter was among the missing, it was now a case of sitting around waiting for news, like so many other families scattered around the nation's capital. As time dragged on it became less and less apparent that she would be found alive.

For James Bowyer he was concerned for his friend Tony Byczkowski, he hadn't showed up for work that day. He did comment on the fact that he may have been on the train but nobody really thought about it, to be honest nobody took notice of how he got to work on a morning. Tony had a girlfriend, Loretta, so maybe he had gone off to spend some time with her. Nobody knew at that time.

That evening James went to his parents' home in Surrey and mentioned the scenario to them, wondering still if Tony had been involved. Not knowing his address to follow it up they would have to sit and wait to see if anything came of it. Although there was nothing that could be done, it would trouble him for the entire weekend until he could get confirmation that he was at work on the Monday.

*

Times journalist Laurence Marks decided to take his hunt for information away from Moorgate station and have a look in the hospitals. He went over to St Bart's where he saw survivors waiting to be seen, talking to some of them, one of them a man around the same age as him. He said he thought that the train had sped up so he grabbed a handle and hung on. The train was packed! It seemed that this incident was turning into a huge story, definitely front page material.

After three hours he decided to find a public phone to ring the news agency with the information that he had gathered. By the time he had relayed all the details that he had, he was then of no further use to the investigation team and decided to return home to his council flat around mid-afternoon. Turning the radio on, he heard the latest developments. So far the information that was coming through was that it was a collision on platform 9 with around seventeen people injured, no fatalities mentioned just yet but there were many still trapped, with the rescuers working tirelessly to free them. It said that the scene of the crash was fifty-two feet below ground and the front half of the train had compressed, police and fire teams fearing many casualties. A phone number came up for any relatives, but Laurence leaned over and switched off the radio. He was now going to get ready to take his wife Sue out for dinner and tell her about the day he'd had at Moorgate.

At 4pm that afternoon the phone rang, it was his stepmother Eve.

"Hello Eve, how are you?"

"Have you heard about the crash?"

"Yes I was sent to cover it," said Laurence.

"I…think your father might have been on the train," she said bleakly.

She then filled him in on the day's events ending with his father Bernard leaving his car at Drayton Park to catch the train to the city. Each day Bernard could be sent to many different kiosks to do stocktaking, so it was only speculation and they started to discuss where he could be.

"Do you know his car registration?" he asked, scribbling down her reply.

At that moment in time she was near Trafalgar Square at a women's wear shop, Laurence sitting at the end of his desk realising that this was probably the longest conversation he had ever had with Eve. After hanging the phone up he realised that he needed to get answers about the crash, as this was fast turning into more than just a newspaper story. The first thing he should do, as it was getting into the evening, was to head down to find his father's car. Heading down to Drayton Park station, he was confronted with silence…and not even 100 yards from the station entrance was his father's Ford Cortina, sat there alone. He went up to it and had a look inside, not sure what he was expecting to see but he did it anyway. By now his dad should have returned a long time ago and driven this car away. It was at this moment that the unthinkable was confirmed. That the man sent to cover the major incident at Moorgate was now more involved in the story than he had ever wanted to be. His father was one of the missing.

*

Ken Thrower was driving his taxi around London as usual that Friday morning. He had arrived at Marylebone station at around 0930 when news came on the radio of the accident at Moorgate. Close by to him was a row of phone boxes and he raced to use the only one that was free. A man was just about to beat him to it when Ken said, "Can I use the phone before you, there has been a rail accident and my father might be involved?" He stepped aside and said, "Yes!" letting Ken in.

As he stood there with the receiver in his hand he cast his mind back to less than two hours before. He had driven down Caledonia Road and as he came to the left turn onto Mackenzie Road he debated whether to turn left to go pick his dad up and save him the train journey or carry on and get to work straight away. The decision to carry on would leave him with a cloud hanging over his head from that day onwards. He might have missed him entirely, a few seconds late or he may have just caught him before he would have got on the train. Either way his thoughts were racing around his head.

He dialled the number for his uncle Leonard who worked at the Daily Mail off Fleet Street. "Have you heard anything about the crash?" said Ken.

"Yes, all the relevant information is coming in, just get down to the office and I'll meet you and we'll take it from there," said his uncle.

The journey down to the offices of the Daily Mail was the longest journey of his life. He kept saying to himself "don't be dead, don't be dead," and although he had no information to say that his father had even got on that particular train, for some reason he had a gut feeling that he was involved. Not just involved, but already dead. He hoped he would be proving his gut feeling to be wrong.

As he arrived at the office the information, so far unconfirmed, was that six people were dead, but Leonard had heard nothing about Thomas Thrower. He didn't stay long as there was nothing there that he didn't already know from the radio in his taxi. He got back in and drove down to his father's house to see his mother at her home in Aubert Court, Highbury. He had his own key so he let himself in, but found nobody at home.

It was around half an hour later that his mother showed up in a very distressed state. She told Ken how she had been on a bus with her sister and had heard two people behind them discussing a major accident at Moorgate. Realising that her husband used that train and that particular station she went straight home. The train had crashed at the same time as when Thomas had usually been on it. At this point she was now frantic with worry.

Together they sat in the living room and put the TV on, searching for more information. With the news reports coming in they saw the emergency number appear across the bottom of the screen. It now became apparent that this number was extremely busy and it seemed very difficult to get through with the amount of worried people ringing to see if their relatives had been involved. London was a big place with thousands of people using the same trains every day. The line would be overwhelmed for a long time yet, so Ken decided to call the doctor instead to see if he could do anything to sedate his mother who was taking the not knowing pretty badly. He agreed to prescribe something to calm her down and Ken raced off to pick up the prescription, stopping to collect the medication on the way. Once she had taken something she seemed to calm down a little, but the worry was evidently still there.

Very soon the phone rang, this time it was Lynda, Ken's wife. She asked if they knew anything yet, but Ken just told her to "prepare for the worst" and hung up. Again they would try ringing the emergency number but once again it was engaged. They would not get through to anybody that day at all. It was just a waiting game now to see what would happen.

*

After seeing the abandoned car at Drayton Park, Laurence Marks headed back home and settled in his armchair. He picked up the phone and dialled the emergency number. Unlike the Throwers, he managed to get through and spoke to a woman. She asked him for details – name, address, telephone number, description, what made him think his father was on the train. He told her that he had set off for work and not come home and his car was still at the station where he had left it.

She asked if he had any distinguishing features.

"A pencil 'tache, wedding ring, blue eyes, a mole…"

"How old?" she asked.

"Sixty-eight but looks younger," was his reply.

She said that she would check the hospitals and get back to him when she had some news.

With nothing else left to do he went over to visit Eve in preparation for breaking the bad news to the family. As predicted the news placards were screaming disaster on every corner. He arrived at her work where she was sitting behind a counter drinking tea. They had a bit of a conversation but she remained calm and said that Bernard had had trouble with his car recently with it not starting. If he had the same problem after work he would have left it in the station and taken the bus back which would have made him very late. "Let's not fear the worst," she said. This was understandable as she had only been married to him for a few months and had already lost her previous husband. Although, she expected him home at around 6-6.30pm, as he would go out and play cards on a Friday night round at his brother's in Essex. With that in mind he rang Eve's number to see if he had arrived home, but nobody was there. So he tried the emergency line again, he got through but the voice on the other end said that they had checked and found nobody in hospital with that description. This was now confusing. If there was no information and he was not on the train, where was he?

He headed back to his flat where his wife had now arrived home from work. She had been on the late shift at the press office at the British Medical Association and was shocked to hear what Laurence had to tell her. She asked if he had informed his brother and sister but he just said that he couldn't do that just yet until it was confirmed that he was definitely on the wrecked train, he might be just simply delayed. The questions kept coming thick and fast with no hope of any answers, but with family members now arriving after hearing the news on the TV and radio there was now no hope of keeping anybody from the truth.

The 9pm news bulletin claimed that all living casualties had been removed from the train wreckage (although this is just before they got the last two people out alive). This led to some hope that he was one of those who was now out since his earlier phone call to the hotline. Again they called the line, but still there was no record of a Bernard Marks being admitted to hospital. While drinking endless cups of tea the sudden thought hit him that the news he would receive would be far from good. The abandoned car; the timings of when he caught the train; nobody hearing from him all day; the fact that he was a creature of habit and wouldn't have just disappeared. By now it was too late to ring Finlays and ask if he had even turned up for work. Grasping at straws they imagined him concussed and walking around London's streets not knowing what had happened. Deep down though, they knew the truth. That Bernard Marks was at this moment still in the train at Moorgate, sat upright, being referred to by firefighters as "The City Gent".

*

All through the night the husband and brother of Shameen Syed waited for news. It was now obvious that she was involved in the crash, and with the news reporting that everybody alive had been brought out, it began to dawn on them that there was no hope left for her. It was late into the night that they got a phone call from the police asking about items of clothing and jewellery that she may have been wearing. They then told them to come at once to St Bart's Hospital.

Heading down as instructed, they arrived as quickly as they could, but all hope finally diminished when they were presented with a number of items. "Do you recognise this?" said the officer. It was her diamond wedding ring. This confirmed everything – she was gone. Tozammel fainted at the shock of realisation and was taken back home to rest. He was given a sedative to calm him down and he fell asleep, not waking up until the Saturday morning.

That morning after, the rest of the family were told the tragic news. It was the phone call to her mother that brought out a very strange tale. During the Friday daytime her mother back in Bangladesh had fallen asleep while reading a book, when she had a dream that Shameen was calling to her, being swept away in a flood and holding out her hand to save her. She jolted awake suddenly and realised it was just a dream. She looked at the clock. It was 2.46pm… …0846 London time.

This wasn't the only strange incident. In London, at the exact time of the crash, Freda Byczkowska was in bed after her son Tony had headed off to work. At the moment of the train crash her legs suddenly shot up the bed, knees bent up to her chest. She had no idea what happened or why she did this in her sleep. In times of disaster, many strange coincidences make an appearance that cannot be explained, leaving those who witness them to let their minds wander.

Chief Inspector Brian Fisher (above and below)

PC Alan Francis around the time of Moorgate

Brian Goodfellow (right)

Crash at Moorgate ©Mirrorpix

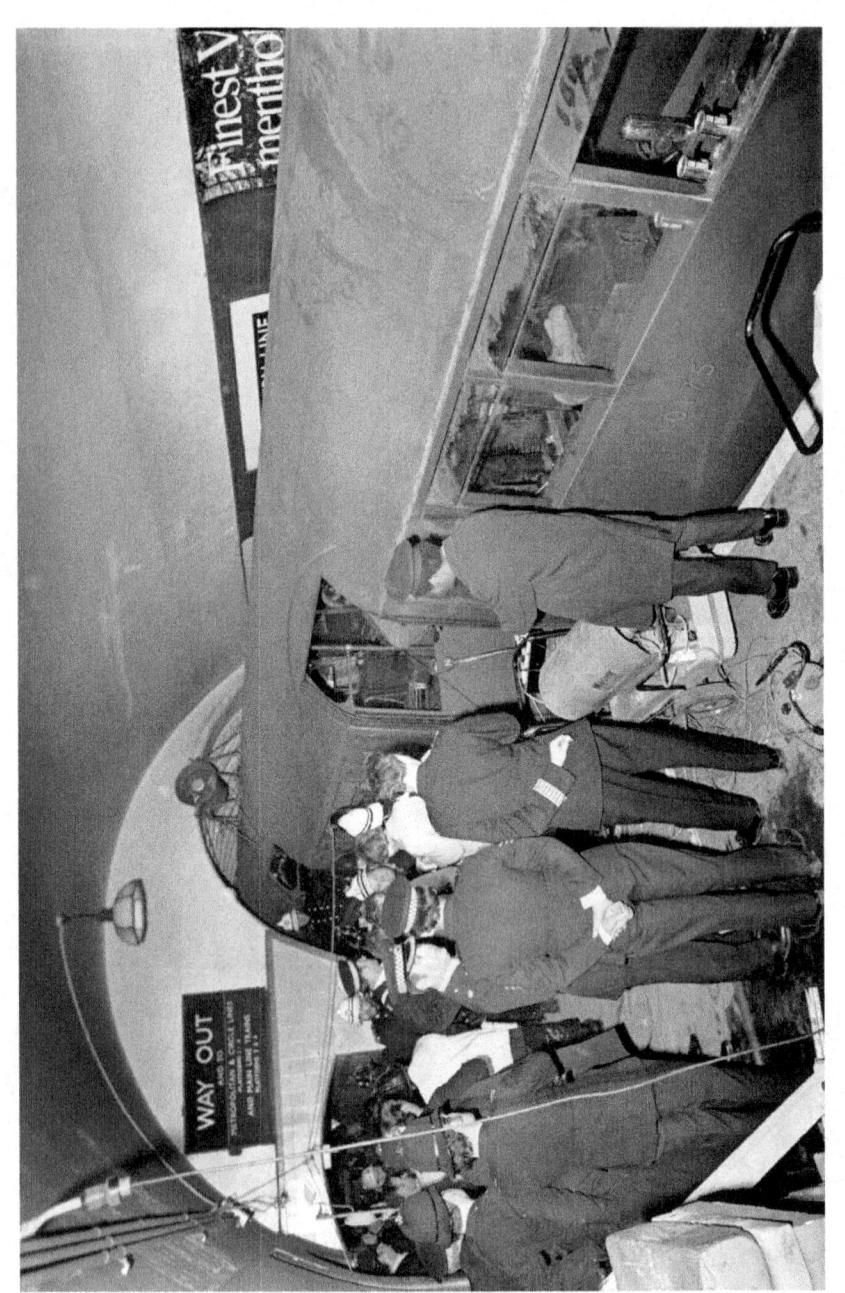

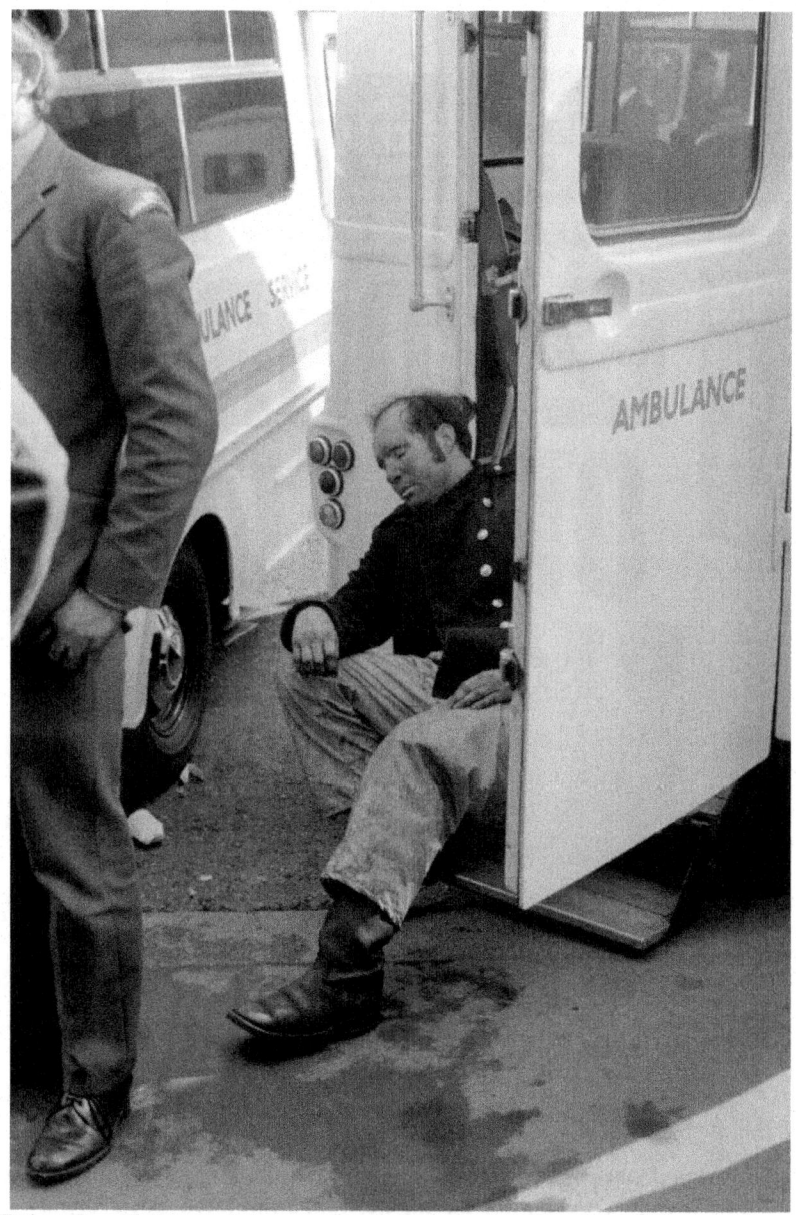

Brian Goodfellow catches a rest after an exhausting day in the wreckage
©Mirrorpix

Daily Mirror front page the day after the crash showing survivor Margaret Liles being rescued after having her foot amputated ©Mirrorpix

102

The London Hospital, now the Royal London Hospital

St Bart's Hospital today

Artwork showing the crash scene

Firemen working in the wreckage of the carriages
©Mary Evans Picture Library

Eileen Smith is led away from the station into the fresh air after spending hours trapped in the wreckage of carriage one.
© Evening News/Rex

6. Days of mourning, Days of grief

Saturday 1st March 1975 dawned with the headlines of the events in London. Most front pages carried the photos of Jeff Benton and Margaret Liles being carried out after the mammoth task to free them. The survivors had all been pulled out of the wreckage of train 272, now the grim task of recovering the bodies awaited. Still nobody was sure how many exactly were in there, it seemed that the list of the missing was growing, then falling, then growing again. For the fire crews and police, their jobs on scene continued. Most papers carried a direct quote from one of the doctors which summed up what they had to go through: "If there's a hell, I've lived to see it." The Queen, who was at the time in Mexico, had sent her condolences for the families.

Brian Fisher had stayed until late at night coordinating the rescues, another officer had taken over during the night and would stay on task through the Saturday. The initial rescue operation had seen seventy-two police officers on scene by 3pm on the Friday, by midnight that had been reduced to around nineteen. The fire crews had nothing much to do now except assist in the recovery operation. Tim Hatton was also back on scene that Saturday morning and had started rigging lighting up in the tunnel for the investigators and recovery teams to work with. With little else left to do he gave a hand lifting the coffins that had been coming and going over the last twenty-four hours. Most firemen were on standby down there just to relieve those in the tunnel as there was still a time limit on how long they could be in there for. The heat was at an unbearable level now and wearing bulky equipment was really not helping, adding to which was the oxyacetylene cutters being used to clear the wreckage.

For fireman Frank David, his wife's father had been taken to hospital the day before in Edinburgh. After he had finished at Moorgate he had to hitch a lift back home in order to get the train to Scotland on the Saturday morning, arriving just in time to say goodbye before he passed away.

Police photographer Adrian Eatwell had been in the station all night, eventually being relieved at 6am. Unfortunately he could only grab around half an hour's sleep at the police station as he was on duty that morning at the station and he was the only person there. After dealing with paperwork on another accident, he eventually got out of work at 2pm and "slept forever".

Andy Day too remained at Moorgate until 8pm on the Saturday when he was finally told to get some rest. After that he would be back at the station for 8am-8pm shifts for as long as the train was still in the tunnel. His colleague Tony Wallis returned for the full Saturday too, as did Peter Simmons who had been at the mortuary when he had heard about the surgery in the tunnel on Margaret Liles. "I remember feeling very angry at the time and thinking that surely they could have got her out without cutting her ankle off. However later when I was taking photographs of the dead bodies in situ I came across the area where the young woman had been trapped and I was speechless with admiration for the skill and courage it must have taken for the surgeon to have carried out the operation, as he would have had to have been upside down to cut her ankle off to free her."

In the meantime Margaret herself was recovering in hospital, even getting a visit from the nurse who had spoken to her in the lift. She told her that unknowingly Margaret had helped her that day. On the day of the crash she had broken up with her boyfriend and was feeling down, but chatting to her laid there after spending twelve hours trapped in a train wreck made her realise just how lucky she was. It made her think of other more important things in life, knowing that dozens of families were now in shock and mourning for the loss of their loved ones, with many more going through treatment to save their lives. That Saturday morning Margaret was taken out of the mixed ward and placed in a side room to recover. She had been the final survivor to be taken to St Bart's.

Francis McPherson had been at the scene of the crash until the Saturday morning, it hit him hard when he returned home that night and he was very upset. After a bath and a large whisky, he went to bed. He would later be called out on Sunday night back to the tunnel, but no bodies were brought out while he was there, so he stuck around for his shift to finish and then returned home.

*

The days following the crash were a mixture of relief for those who had lived through the terror, and grief for those who had lost their family members. It was bad enough realising that people were missing, but it was even worse when there was no information available to work with. By now there were dozens of bodies still trapped in train 272. The firemen were fighting to remain able to continue their job without passing out with the incredible heat. For those above ground waiting for news it was a whole different kind of pain. For the family of Stephen Payne it was confirmed that his body was recovered at 2am on Saturday 1st March. They had got that final confirmation in a phone call; he had been badly crushed in the impact.

The rescue operation was officially at an end, it was now a recovery mission for those who had not been so lucky, and a search for evidence that would explain what had gone so wrong. Many families still hadn't had confirmation that their loved ones were or were not involved in the crash; in the first thirty-six hours or so over 800 people had rung the emergency number given out by police, many of them being left without any news at all.

That morning as the sun came up, families were being told about the efforts overnight to recover their loved ones. Janet King had two police officers come round to tell her that her fiancé Peter had been recovered from the second carriage. She found out later that he had died of cerebral contusion (injury to the brain). She would be grateful in the long run that he had died on impact and not suffered. "Peter was at the front of the second carriage so died because of the impact itself. I don't know this but I suspect he was already standing, ready to get off the train."

It wasn't so easy for the Throwers, who by now had most of the family round after they had been called with the news overnight. By now fewer people were ringing the emergency helpline so it was easier for Ken to finally get through. Despite the information he gave them, there were definitely no survivors by that name and description and nobody (so far) who had been brought out of the wreckage. Even when he rang on the Sunday he got through no problem, just to be told there was still no information. "Are you sure he was on the train?" he would be asked.

*

At 7am on the Saturday, daylight was creeping in through the windows of the home of Laurence Marks. He woke up after a long night of worrying, not remembering going to sleep so he would have most likely just dozed off without realising. He had not eaten since breakfast the day before, but he was not hungry and just kept on making cups of tea instead.

On a normal Saturday morning his dad would arrive ready to go and watch Arsenal play, they would walk together for the fifteen minutes it would take to get to the stadium down the road. This was the only real thing he and his father had in common, between Sunday and Friday they barely spoke to each other. It was only their love of the game that kept them talking.

At this point they had a visit from a woman who said that she knew his father had been killed. A man named George Tisser had seen Bernard get on the train and depart for Moorgate, he had got on the train behind, which was then stopped from entering the station because of the crash up ahead, and considering platform 10 was closed due to engineering work, he said that the passengers were forced to depart the train and walk along the tracks to climb up onto platform 10 and depart the station, keeping out of the way of the rescue workers. This news confirmed his worst fear.

Suddenly there was a ring on the doorbell again, this time when he opened it there stood a uniformed police officer. "May I come in?" he said, removing his helmet.

"Would you like a cup of tea?" asked Laurence, by now probably sick of the sight of tea. The officer politely declined and instead pulled out his notebook. He then recited what he had written down.

"Your father Bernard Marks was removed from the wreckage of the train at 0430 this morning. I am terribly sorry…he is dead."

The shock was naturally there but it was also a relief that the waiting was over. The police officer did not have a good day ahead of him, he had now told three families that their loved ones were dead, he had two more left to do. Eve offered him a brandy but he again declined as he was on duty and had to leave and carry on his sad tasks.

The first thing Laurence did now was to telephone his sister, but as soon as she heard the tone of his voice she knew what had happened. He asked if Alex, his brother-in-law, would come with him to the City of London mortuary to identify the body. He agreed and they went down together, Alex making the positive ID for him. In accordance with Jewish tradition he had to be buried within twenty-four hours, so they would have to make arrangements for the funeral straight away.

Leaving the mortuary they saw a woman in the waiting room inconsolable. He offered her a tissue as he went past, but like everybody else there was nothing anybody could do to make the pain go away. He started ringing around one or two of his father's friends as well as the Finsbury Park synagogue, which Bernard had been a member of before he died. Eve organised the funeral at Waltham Cross Jewish Cemetery and everybody who needed to be told was told.

That Sunday morning, the family gathered at Laurence's flat in disbelief. People were saying how much of a tragedy it was, how Bernard was very fit for his age. How could this happen? Laurence had fits of guilt over their last conversation the week before when he had let himself into his flat. Despite their differences, his father was a popular man, he had plenty of friends, colleagues, family, and even members of a youth club that he had run turned up to pay their respects.

So with people still trapped in the wreckage of the train underground, the funeral of Bernard Marks took place. This had, however, also turned into another family argument. Eve wanted him to be buried in a reserved plot with her, not near Laurence's mother where it had always thought he would be laid to rest. Nobody had the energy to argue with her and they just let things take their course. On the day of the funeral there were news cameras at the gate, the irony being that Bernard had never been in the news during his entire life, but now his death was making the front pages of the papers. Laurence walked up to the camera crews and asked them to respect the family's privacy. "I too am a journalist and covered the crash…please leave us in peace." After the ceremony at Waltham Cross, a black Daimler drove them back to Eve's home for the wake; it was on this occasion that he was invited into her home for the first time.

*

The operation to recover the bodies of those still missing would take several days, the train had to be taken apart piece by piece to get to them, acrow props holding up the parts that hung over. Carriage three was taken back first to reveal the mangled wrecks of cars one and two. The work was slow and painstaking with the firemen now able to freely use cutting equipment to take away whole sections of the train at a time, each section being pulled away and photographed, as were the dead passengers and their possessions. The heat and smell were getting really bad, firefighters were wearing masks while they worked, alternating between each other still. Railway workers were on scene working just as hard and giving assistance to the fire crews with what they could. These men would stay there till the bitter end.

By Sunday the train had been stuck in the tunnel for nearly three days, and a decontamination point had to be set up due to the threat of disease.

The main coaches were starting to be pulled out, bodies being revealed; with the time and the heat the danger was all too real. For fireman Tim Hatton this was his last day down there, at his station they would send half the shift over to assist at Moorgate while the other half stayed back at the station for any call-outs. Thankfully he was due a couple of days off, well deserved after the horrendous images that now stuck in his mind.

Tony Wallis would be back on the Saturday taking more photographs for the investigation teams, but not the Sunday. Brian Tibbenham was on scene for the next few days but it was all routine work, the press still having a presence outside, so his job was just making sure that it was all kept under control with regular updates on progress.

The weekend TV news reports showed the public how difficult it was for the fire brigades to reach the trapped victims and that the temperature was so high they had to work in shifts of around fifteen to twenty minutes before they would become exhausted and have to come out. On the Monday morning, 3rd March, Police Officer Alan Francis took a telephone call from Briton, the engineering firm, stating that they had the answer to at least one of the problems. The managing director stated that they could be there in just three hours with a flexible 18-inch diameter tube system which would supply fresh air from the street down to the platform, therefore reducing the temperature and giving the crews clean air.

After expressing his gratitude, he put him in touch with the police "Mivvi Van" which had direct contact with the London Transport engineers. The offer was immediately accepted and a huge fan in a one metre cube cage was installed in the booking hall, tubes connecting it to the centre of the escalator and down to the working fire crews. The heat problem was now becoming at least bearable and offered better working conditions to the exhausted fire crews.

Tim Hatton went back to the station in time to see the night shifts come on at around 5pm on the Sunday. Covered in dirt, he would chat to them and brief them on developments and what they had achieved during the day. There was no official debrief, it was simply back to work as normal.

Brian Goodfellow returned to the tunnel for the following four days after the crash, working two day and two night shifts. Entering the carriages he again saw the woman with the auburn hair before she was gently removed and taken away to be identified. Standing on top of carriage one he was looking for members of his team when he shone the torch down and saw a sea of faces looking back up at him. With the silence from inside, the scene was one of absolute horror.

By now it was the afternoon of only the second day and the crews were relieving each other more regularly and coming from all around London to assist. Hot cutting was started but this was using up precious air, and smoke was starting to build up. They had to stop until they had rigged the extractor fans to clear the smoke, in the meantime medical teams were setting up their decontamination centre. Masks, which had a strong smell of rose petals, were handed out to the fire crews. This didn't go with what they were seeing and started to mess with their heads, so several people took them off and carried on working without them.

*

The weekend had come and gone with still no word for several families. The Monday dawned and, although people were clinging to hope, it was getting less and less likely that people like David Wilson would be found alive. His family knew he would have been stood in the most vulnerable part of the train waiting to leave by the front passenger door as was his routine. Then the inevitable call came that brought news that a body which might be David's had been taken out of the wreckage and was now with the coroner. He was positively identified as David by his dental records due to the large amount of treatment he had had on his teeth over the last few years. This saved two family members having to view his body which had lain in the tunnel for three days.

Less than a mile away James Bowyer realised that his friend Tony Byczkowski had not turned up for work again. By now his mother Freda had rung the office to inquire if he had been there on the Friday. After he had failed to come home from work that night she didn't know what had happened until the news reports came on that evening about the crash. She had spent the entire weekend in distress, not knowing anything and having the most terrible thoughts. When she had confirmation that he did not turn up Friday, nor had he turned up today, this confirmed for her that Tony was on the train. James was shocked like everybody else there, he looked around and saw grown men openly crying with grief at the loss of one of their colleagues. The disaster had already hit London hard, especially in the city where so many of the victims came from. His father was the senior partner in the firm so he made it his business to offer help to Tony's family as much as he could and he visited his grieving mother on several occasions. He would later assist her in getting a lawyer in order to fight for better compensation.

*

For Ken Thrower the frustration on the Monday was just as bad as it had been all weekend. He was getting straight through on the helpline but was receiving the same answer to his questions, being told simply, "I think you have got it wrong, he is not on the train."

He had spent the last few days visiting the hospitals looking for his father, although deep down he seemed to know that he wouldn't be there. He headed down to the mortuary to ask if anybody new had been brought in. They thought he was just out to have a look at the bodies thinking he was some kind of ghoul. "You're not going to have a look!" they would say to him. He just looked at them and asked if there was anybody fitting his father's description. Again the answer was no.

However, it was around midday on the Tuesday that he got the phone call that ended all this. It was a police officer asking him to come down to the mortuary near Moorgate station. By this point he knew that his search for answers was almost at an end. He headed down to the mortuary at Milton Court and was called into the coroner's office with his brother Peter and uncle Len.

The first thing they were asked was what he was wearing at the time. They said he would have had a dark brown trench coat, probably woollen socks. Then a number of personal items were produced, this included money that had obviously been chemically treated to clean it before it was shown to them.

They confirmed that the few items, a special sentimental watch and a pen, were that of Thomas Thrower, but it wasn't enough for Len who then said that he would like to see his body. They said it wouldn't be advisable but he persisted. He was told quite frankly, "Look, you've been through a war, you have seen a few sights, you don't want to see this. If you go in there the smell will stick with you." Ken realised what he was saying, so he turned to his uncle and said, "Len, you don't need to go in," and persuaded him to leave it be.

As they turned to leave at 2pm that afternoon, Peter turned to the coroner with a heavy heart and simply said, "Will you thank the emergency services for us," before walking out of the office. The next stop was to go home and start planning Thomas's funeral; this was going to be a big event for the area with the amount of things he was involved in, so they informed the police that there may be a lot of cars attending which they duly made a note of.

Tuesday was also the day the search teams found the body of Terry Hall. The news of her death had aged her parents ten years in just a few days. They had received word of the confirmation that morning, their dad and 20-year-old brother Tony driving down to the mortuary. Tony had literally only just come home on leave from the army on Friday and had actually read about the disaster on the train home in the Evening Standard. Parking on double yellow lines, Tony would stay in the car while his dad went in. When he went inside and confirmed who he was, they wouldn't let him see her body. Like Thomas Thrower, she was identified by her belongings – a set of earrings that her mother had bought her and a St Christopher, together with the various contents of her handbag which were confirmed as being hers. It was here that Terry's father was told there and then that he had to make up his mind whether she was to be buried or cremated. Being taken aback by the sudden decision he had to make, he decided burial and quickly left to make the journey back home. When he returned home and talked about it they decided they wanted a cremation but they were told it was too late by then to change their minds. They have never been told why they had to make this decision so quickly and why they couldn't change it.

*

At St Bart's Hospital on Monday 3rd March there came an unexpected visitor. Prince Charles made an appearance, arriving without prior notice as he didn't want a fuss and just wanted to see the survivors and offer some words of comfort. There were fourteen injured survivors still in St Bart's at this point and another fifteen at the London Hospital in Whitechapel. One of those in St Bart's was Margaret Liles who seemed to be a lot more cheerful now she was sitting upright in bed and smiling for the cameras. People visiting her would never guess from her attitude that she had been in a terrible disaster and had suffered the loss of a limb whilst trapped in the carriage for hours.

Andy Day would be at the crash site for five days, each one being a twelve hour shift. He would arrive at the scene and report to the senior police officer who introduced him to an engineer.

"We're going to work our way through," he said. "As I pull bits out, you take photos. Or if I can't pull things out then photograph in situ." With a plan in progress, the men got to work.

The number of photographs taken easily ran into the thousands: colour slides and black and white images of anything and everything; bodies, body parts, wreckage, firemen working, equipment. Even though only a few hundred were ever used in the investigation it still needed to be done. He even went to take photos of the surrounding buildings next to the station showing the locations of police vans and ambulances. The upcoming inquiry may want to check the tiniest of details, so everything had to be fully documented and recorded.

After several days of wearing overalls and face masks, he would return home each night feeling very dehydrated. Up until now he only ever really had to deal with road accidents and suicides, but coming across fifteen to twenty dead bodies in a railway carriage is something that he couldn't forget about so easily. On the first day of his having been down there his wife poured him a big drink and told him to try and put it out of his mind. She told the children to leave their daddy alone for a few days so he could rest and be away from any stress. She was a nurse so she knew exactly what to do to help him. After stripping off his clothes at the door, he would take a long bath, throwing his garments away because of the lingering smell from the tunnel sticking to them.

Gary Thomas wasn't on scene again for several days, when he did return he was tasked to be part of the RVP (rendezvous point) team, keeping people out of the way and letting those down who were authorised. It was now agreed to let him take junior ITN reporter Martin Lewis down to view the scene. With his news cameraman close by, Gary gave them both a brief on what they were going to see down at the platform. "When you go down there you might see things that you don't want to see," he told them, before leading them down the staircase, avoiding the ventilation tubes, down to the platform to the scene of the crash. After taking a short time viewing the carnage that was still apparent after the weekend, they got the information they required and departed back up top. Looking at his shoulder number (208), the reporter just said, "Two, oh, eight...I'll remember you. The next time you tell me not to go somewhere, I'm not going." He was visibly shocked by what he had seen down there; by now the fire teams were used to the scene and had it mapped out, imprinted on their minds. For the civilian journalist, he never returned to the scene.

By now loads of random stories were in the press about what had gone on. The Sun reported that Margaret Liles had been fitted with a microphone to talk to the rescuers, but this was false. Unconfirmed reports and rumours circulated that a young lad had survived and both his parents had died. Another guy was found with several wallets in his possession, a possible train pickpocket. A small child was amongst those killed. All of these stories were most likely not true, they certainly appear in no official publication or report and, like the conspiracy theories that were already brewing up about the cause of the crash, they would have no evidence to support any of them.

By now specialist equipment was being brought in from all over London. Forge of Dagenham had a spray paint shop and they donated piles of face masks for the search teams. The RAF came up with foot baths which could be filled with disinfectant for the teams to walk through to disinfect the soles of their boots. Breweries like Whitbread in the City of London sent beer down for the lads to have a drink to at least give them a change from water now the air temperature had been sorted out. The Salvation Army, WRVS and the First Aid Nurses Yeomanry were all still there helping sort out tea and sandwiches for the workers. At the height of the searching there could be anything up to 200-300 people all in the station working, with three separate police forces – British Transport Police, the Metropolitan and City of London – all working together. Conditions were getting worse as the smell of the bodies was now so strong it was clinging to the clothes of the crews, adding to it the hot burning smell from the angle grinding. The temperature was still very high despite the air conditioning, but by now four to five days had passed with victims still at the front of carriage one trapped in the heat.

*

Chris Robertson had been visiting Marian over the weekend and had got quite close to her brother. They decided to go for a drink to get together and to talk about things. It was quite traumatic for both of them, but they each had the comradeship of the other and knew what each other was talking about. Chris was desperate to know the extent of her injuries and whether her condition would get any worse. As information about the crash was getting back to them via the papers and news reports, that gave them other aspects of the incident to talk about and discuss what had gone on. This helped them in many ways come to terms with almost losing somebody they both loved.

Eileen Smith remained in the London Hospital for eight days before being sent home. When she was discharged the hospital gave her a watch as part of her possessions. When pointing out that this was given to her by mistake, they said it was entangled in her hair when she arrived. A few weeks later she handed it in to Wood Street Police Station, never finding out if it was ever claimed.

It was only when she returned home that she finally found out what had really gone on at Moorgate. The nurses at the hospital had kept all the news away from her while she recovered, she could not leave her bed due to her injuries and never went into the day room. Upon realisation of the extent of the crash, she had a breakdown. Not in her wildest imagination did she realise the extent of what she had been involved in.

*

In the meantime the investigators were recovering the last of the bodies, and slowly but surely the remains of the train were pulled back inch by inch revealing the driver's cab. Both Tony Wallis and Adrian Eatwell got the first photographs of the state of the cab and the position of the driver. Within seconds of seeing the body of Leslie Newson it became clear that he had not applied the brakes. Various news reports say that the driver's cab, normally 3ft 6ins deep, had been compressed to anything between 4 and 11 inches.

Engineers swarmed over the equipment and it didn't take long to see that the brakes *had* in fact been applied at the last second, but this was down to an automatic stopping system triggered by the sand drag hitting the lever on the front bogey. This reset automatically when the wheels came away from the bottom of the carriage. It didn't take long though for people to see this as more than it actually was. Equipment was looked at by forensics and engineers who found that the train itself was in good working order, in fact some equipment was still serviceable!

At 2050 on the night of Tuesday 4th March the final trapped body, that of driver Les Newson, was carefully removed from his position in the cab. He was taken away to be examined by the mortuary team who were already waiting. It had taken almost five solid days to recover his body, all this time his family grieving for his loss, but unable to have a death certificate until his actual death was confirmed by a doctor. Most death certificates would say 4th March for those trapped, because technically they would still be classed as living until proven otherwise.

The officer working on the mortuary team assisted Professor Keith Simpson with his examinations, sitting on the end of the slab writing notes on his direction. One night he did nine post mortems, finishing at around 0400 one morning. That particular night he got a lift home and walked into his garden, switching on his torch. Suddenly his Light Sussex cockerel went berserk leading to his hens doing the same. Thankfully he had good understanding neighbours!

The City of London coroner was Dr David Paul. A man described as cool, calm and collected, as a coroner should be. He was allegedly having steak and chips without a care in the world as the train driver's body was finally being released; not a man to let his work affect his life, otherwise he wouldn't last two minutes. He would work with his team examining the teeth against dental records, photographing faces and taking fingerprints. One night duty officer was tasked to remove the clothes of a man who had been in the carriage for several days, the smell alone was making him retch. He wasn't sick and continued doing it despite feeling like he wanted to be. By the time he had finished he had earned the respect of his colleagues who looked on at him ready to take over should he find it too much.

Doing twelve hour shifts in there from 7pm to 7am would take its toll on you if you didn't keep taking breaks. At one point during the night somebody said they were hungry and all of a sudden the rest of the mortuary team felt the same. It had most likely been many hours since having a proper meal, and the teams needed to keep their energy up. Out of nowhere cheese rolls were obtained, bearing in mind this was during the night. This was most likely from the Salvation Army or one of the other voluntary brigades that were still on task. Looking back now, it seemed strange to take a bite out of a sandwich, put it down and carry on with the note taking and post mortem work. But in the last few days, eating here seemed the least of their concerns.

A London Transport official came to the Newson house to give them the confirmation that Les had been brought out. It would be nice to say that it would be almost the end of the story for them, after the funeral, but because Les had been the driver his body was now subjected to the usual post mortem and a series of tests to find out what had gone on with him in the hours leading up to the crash.

The press seemed to be constantly hounding them, their address was published in the newspapers and half a dozen people seemed to be always there outside waiting for them every time they left the building. Sandra and her husband, with their baby son Robert, would live at Helen's for the next few months. Helen was taking it very badly, she felt like she was in a daydream and would never recover from the impact of the trauma suffered. These press reporters would keep coming round for a year after, especially on the anniversaries. They would pester the Newsons for a story shouting, "The public have the right to know!" To which they turned to them and said, "But we are the public and we have a right to privacy!" As usual the press did not respect their wishes and waited for the story that may or may not make them their headlines.

*

The body of Shameen Syed was taken to the East London Mosque where she remained for three days. Her husband Tozammel was fully supported at his work to take whatever time off he needed and to make sure he kept in touch with them with updates. They offered him a month's leave and were very understanding and cooperative. On Wednesday 5th March he had the sad duty of escorting his wife's body back to Bangladesh. Her brother Farhad needed to stay in London for his studies but he had been a big help to him in the days after the crash. Although younger than his wife he was emotionally very strong. As the plane carrying the sad cargo touched down in Dhaka, the coffin of Shameen Syed was taken away and at 1.30 that afternoon prayers were said at the funeral. She was buried straight away at the Banani graveyard in her home town. What Tozammel didn't know until her death was that he would be burying two people that day. Shameen Syed's post mortem had shown she had been pregnant. Echoing back her final letter, she kept her promise in death that she would make her mother a surprise visit in March. It was a surprise that nobody wanted in this context.

*

At Moorgate station the work had been going on now for over five solid days. On the early morning of Wednesday 5th March the fire brigade control unit packed up and left the scene. The rescue and recovery mission was now officially over. The number of dead had been confirmed as forty-one, with dozens of others in hospital with injuries ranging from critical to minor. Only time would tell what would be in store for those people. It was now down to the investigators to pick up the task of finding out what happened in those final seconds of train 272's journey.

7. Questions and Answers

No sooner had the bodies been recovered than the next stage began into finding the cause of the crash. What could possibly make a seemingly good train with a seemingly cautious driver suddenly slam headlong into the wall at great speed? Was the train faulty? First indications said no. The wreckage proved that all mechanics were in good working order at the time of the crash, the normal daily inspections had been carried out and the braking system was said to be almost good enough to re-use! Was the driver aware of what he was doing and where he was heading? Did anybody try to stop the impending collision? Was there enough time to react even if anybody did want to stop the train? This and hundreds more questions needed to be answered. Several police forces and fire brigades worked closely with London Transport to begin the mammoth task of examining the wreckage, interviewing survivors, examining bodies and taking statements from eyewitnesses.

Adrian Eatwell was at the post mortem of Les Newson. He could see that there were a lot of people eager to inspect the body and closely examine their findings. British Transport and City of London Police were there with two pathologists, Professor Keith Simpson and Professor James Cameron of the London Hospital. Sixty-seven year old Professor Simpson had dealt with many famous headline-hitting cases including the victims of the Bethnal Green tube disaster in 1943, those of acid bath serial killer John Haigh, also Sandra Rivett (murdered by Lord Lucan in 1974) and George Cornell (killed by gangster Ronnie Kray in 1966). Neither man was a stranger to cases such as this and with hard work they should have this case closed easily enough.

When they inspected the heart one of them was heard to remark, "His heart is better than mine!" meaning he was in good health. Samples of his blood were taken and analysed in a lab, but results were not very conclusive due to the fact that the heat factor in the tunnel, together with the natural decomposition of a body, left many people disagreeing with each other.

In the meantime Adrian and his photography team went back into what was left of the wreckage to continue photographing everything they could find. He would stay there until the Thursday as they were dragging the final parts of the train out, taking snaps every step of the way. Nothing should be missed, every piece of equipment, every dial and button position, every pipe and wire. Different angles were shot in case they were needed, inside the tunnel, the train, inside the tunnel looking out of the train. At the end of his job he handed everything over to the investigation teams to use and left the decisions to them over what would be useful. Other members of Adrian's team went back to the mortuary to help with the fingerprinting and identifications. Once the rescue and recovery operation had been completed it was handed over from the City of London Police to the British Transport Police who would take it from there. It was now a case of preparing the line for reopening to normal passenger trains, as by now it had been closed to traffic for the best part of a week.

Survivor Barry Coppock was spoken to by the police, who asked him questions about the driver and the journey. He just said that he didn't notice anything as he got on at Highbury and he would have had no reason to look at him. As the platform there was on the right hand side, Newson would have been on the opposite side to him anyway. He didn't notice the guard at the back either, nor did he notice anything unusual about the journey.

*

On 19th March a service was delivered at St Paul's Cathedral to remember the victims of the disaster, led by the Bishop of London, the Right Rev. Gerald Ellison. Among those attending were the Wilsons, Paynes, Wonderlings, Donovans, and hundreds of others, united in a common act of grief in remembering the forty-one people who had died. Guests included London Transport Chairman Kenneth Robinson, Greater London Council Chairman Lord Pitt and the Lord Mayor of London Sir Murray Fox. Three days previously another service, this one a civic service to remember the citizens of the Borough of Islington, had been held in St Mary's Church on Upper Street.

But the death toll in the Moorgate disaster would not stay at forty-one for long. Jeff Benton, the last person to be pulled out alive, had been laid in bed for several weeks. The day after the crash his brother Keith had come to see him, at this point he was very agitated, still with soot on his face from the tunnel, and confessed that he was worried that they were going to amputate his legs. His lower body was in a bad way, his legs had been crushed and the hospital had got him to sign a form. Looking distressed he just said, "You're not going to cut my legs off are you?"

The morning following the disaster, he chatted briefly to his wife Val although he was in great pain. The plasters had to be removed from his legs as there was concern of gangrene setting in. The lack of blood circulation for such a long time while trapped in the wreckage had created additional problems and his body was unable to fight back. The antibiotics were increased and he was placed in ICU and then a few days later, he was placed into a "tunnel" to try and clear the skin of the infection. Val was getting more and more worried as time went on. "There was an occasion when the doctors requested I sign a form to agree to the amputation of his legs from the knee down. After I signed this, I remember going home and thinking, "OK we can cope with this, we can sell our terrace house and buy a cottage in the countryside and we will work together and accept that he will be in a wheelchair, but at least we will be together and have each other."

Their father worked as a tailor in Tottenham Court Road and would go to Whitechapel every day to see him. Initially his parents and brother would go in there to see him together, spending around forty-five minutes to an hour talking to him. He opened up to them about what it was like during the long hours trapped in the dark. "It was horrible, hot, pitch black, screaming, moaning, then silence, then moaning again." As the day went on he lay there in his hospital bed in a lot of pain, his upper body barely having a mark on it, but for the lower body and internally it was a different story. His right leg was broken at the femur, and below the knee was entirely crushed. He was then sedated to the point of total unconsciousness, and all the nurses could do now was to tell his family to keep talking to him as he might still be able to hear them. It was around a week before his face and hair was finally washed of all the dirt, all this time he would just lay there still and silent, oblivious to the drama going on around him.

Jeff's muscle tissue now had poison in it due to all the injuries, and his kidneys needed to be flushed out. He became dehydrated and the doctors were fighting to chemically battle with the organs to keep the poison from getting into his system. This was known as "crush syndrome" and there had been very few cases since the end of the Second World War where this had happened. The doctors and nurses fought hard to save his life for several weeks.

On the night of 26th March he had visits from his wife Val, his brother Keith and a boss from his work called Wilson who had come down from Hertfordshire. As they sat in the nearby waiting room ready to go in, they were startled by the sudden sound of various buzzers starting to go off, prompting doctors and nurses to rush into Jeff's room. It wasn't long after that one of them approached the family and told them the bad news. "I'm very sorry, we've lost him." The poison had got into his system and after a huge fight with the elements he had lost his fight for life and died. The three of them were left to console each other where they stood, before Wilson drove them to Keith's parents to break the news. His mother had seen Jeff only the once on the morning after the crash and had not been to see him again, she found it too hard to see her son laid there and wanted to remember him for how he was. Secretly they had suspected all along that he wasn't going to make it, although after several operations they still had glimmers of hope. Now all that hope had been dashed and Jeff had become another victim of the Moorgate disaster. Doctors said that if he had have pulled through he would have been psychologically scarred, in days when counselling virtually didn't exist. He had left a widow, parents, a brother and two younger sisters aged twelve and nine to mourn his passing.

It was a short time after that the family was walking through Wood Green Shopping Centre and they saw Moorgate survivor Margaret Liles. Keith introduced himself to her as Jeff's brother and they warmed to each other straight away. She asked how he was and was shocked to hear that he had survived the crash but had died weeks later. She later sent a wreath to the family with the message. "To my 13-hour friend."

London Transport paid for the funeral; the family had previously been worried about it as they were not rich by any standards, but thankfully they came to their aid and his life was celebrated at Southgate Crematorium church on 1st April, with hundreds of people paying tribute. The front room of Keith's house was full of flowers, and teachers from his old Bishopswood Secondary School were there. There were so many well-wishers and mourners that the crowd spilled out into the churchyard! With a light shower of snow, Keith went about shaking hands with people and thanking them for their support. He had been close to his brother and had a lot of friends. They all went away for drinks after the service and before long the day had drawn to a close.

*

The inquest was moved from the initial date of 15th May 1975 and brought forward to 14th April at the Livery Hall in Guildhall. Each family member received a letter explaining this change and it also told them that they were well within their rights to cross-examine any witnesses themselves or through legal representation. This change of date was due to the size of the Hall and that it was available only at that time, the space needed in order to accommodate the vast number of people who would be turning up. The inquest would be led by Dr David Paul, who was a medical doctor and a lawyer as well as Coroner for the City of London, and who had already done a vast amount of work during the recovery period in identification and evidence collecting. So as to not meet any of the critical witnesses or relatives in the local area he would dine in a private room at Wood Street Police Station where the force would provide him with a meal and a bit of quiet in between sittings. Alan Francis would remember him as "a very jovial man, we enjoyed looking after him."

It was Dr Paul who said that the investigation was going the wrong way round, the inquiry had already taken place and had heard all the evidence, but this should have taken place AFTER the inquest. To have both the inquest and inquiry wrapped up within two months was simply too fast. But this did not suggest that the work done by either was open to question, in fact it was done professionally and thoroughly. In some ways though it was too quick for many of those giving evidence who were still grieving their loss. However, the inquest was to start without delay and the jury of nine men was seated in court as the first evidence was shown and the witnesses took the stand, press reporters gathering to write down everything that would be said. Around sixty relatives of those killed were there to hear the inquest, which had sixty-one witnesses to call over a three to four day period.

The first evidence to be heard was concentrated on the driver, and the two pathologists, Professors Cameron and Simpson, spoke of the injuries sustained to driver Newson and the fact he was found consistent with the positions of where his hands should be on the controls.

Guard Robert Harris took the stand and admitted that he was not in the right place where he should have been and couldn't even tell what speed the train was going at as he said he trusted the driver and went to look for a newspaper. He did, however, mention an incident around four to five days before the crash where Newson accidentally overshot the platform, at which point Les had simply said that he had misjudged. Harris was witness number thirty and he was examined by Dr Paul on the moments leading up to the fatal Moorgate crash on 28th February.

Q - Did you signal the driver to move out of Old Street?
A - Yes.
Q - What did you do then?
A - As we were leaving the platform I went to the back of the cab.
Q - What was the purpose of that?
A - To see if there was a paper there.
Q - Are you familiar with the Rule Book?
A - Yes.
Q - Have you got a copy of that Rule Book here? May I refer you to page 24 of the Appendix S11, of the Appendix to the Rule Book, 1969, under the heading "Responsibility of Guards".
A - I have got it, yes.
Q - Are you familiar with the Rule Book?
A - Well, I have read it a couple of times.
Q - Well, if you look at page 40, under the section labelled W12, maybe you would be good enough to read it to my jury.
A - "Guards are not permitted to occupy passenger seats whilst working trains. The guard must ride at his proper position and, except in emergency, not leave that position whilst the train is in motion. When it is necessary for the guard of an air worked door to leave his position for any reason except when being relieved at an intermediate station, he must remove his position switch key and take it with him."
Q - Was there an emergency which caused you to leave your station?
A - No.
Q - You left to get a paper.
A - That is correct.

Dr. Paul had made his point. Later on, discussing the crash, he brought up the overshoot incident.

Q - At any time, between your journey from Old Street to Moorgate, were you in a position to apply the emergency handle at your control position?
A - No.
Q - Were you in a position to apply an emergency handle at any other position?
A - Yes.
Q - Did you, at any time, consider doing so?
A - Well, seeing as I never knew we were entering Moorgate I wouldn't

dream of it, no.

Q - Do you remember any other occasion when a train driven by Mr Newson overshot?

A - I believe, yes.

Q - When was that?

A - It was either Monday or Tuesday before this particular Friday.

Q - Did you report it or note it in your journal?

A - No.

Q - Why was that?

A - Well, there was no harm done. We didn't overshoot enough to cause any inconvenience and I didn't think it was necessary.

Q - Did you speak to Mr Newson about the overshoot…on the Monday or Tuesday before this incident?

A - When we got to Moorgate I said, "What happened there then?"…and Leslie said…he said, "Just misjudged it. I dropped the handle but it didn't stop as quick as I thought."

That overshoot was the distance of an entire carriage in an open tunnel. Going back to the crash several days later, the newspapers reported several of the train's passengers giving concern over the driver. Mrs Frances Rhodes had said that the driver seemed in a hurry. She claims to have seen Les walking to his cab before its journey from Drayton Park and said, "It seemed to me he shut the door rather loudly. And as soon as the door of the cab was closed, the train doors shut as well and the train seemed to pull away more quickly than usual. I said to myself, 'He's in a hurry this morning.'"

Another passenger, Mrs Daphne Poutney, said she got on the train at Highbury & Islington and an elderly woman was complaining that people had been thrown off balance as the train pulled up. She said she noticed the same when they pulled up to Essex Road and Old Street stations too.

Relief signalman Walter Wade said he saw Newson on the morning of the crash and he seemed quite normal. Whether these observations were simply a case of over thinking about an event afterwards, knowing that the train later crashed, is something that only these witnesses themselves know. There were plenty of people who made that regular journey who saw absolutely no difference to any other trip they had made.

*

The journalists covering the story for the papers were not looked at with any joy by the families of those attending. Tony Byczkowski's sister June was there every day and found one of them very insensitive, referring to her brother as "just one of many".

On day two of the inquest the focus was once again back on the train's driver. Dr Anne Robinson, a senior lecturer of forensic medicine at the London Hospital, took the stand and said to the court that she had conducted tests on several of Newson's organs and had found the alcohol content significantly greater than that of eight others who had died close by. She gave the figures of 80 milligrams out of 100 millilitres, which at the time was the level at which road drivers could be prosecuted for drink-driving. She said to a shocked courtroom that this level of alcohol was the equivalent of having downed five single shots of whisky.

When the court was being told of the alcohol content of Les Newson's blood, the entire stream of news reporters got up and ran out to make calls to their work to tell them this incredible development. What they didn't hear was the next part of the evidence which suggested that the levels were no greater than what was to be expected of a body fermenting in the hot tunnel for four days at extreme heat. But by then it was too late. No sooner had the words left the lips, than the newspapers were having a field day. It was obvious to some that a drunk train driver had crashed the train, mystery solved. Another theory that was brought out at the same time was that Les could have been mesmerised by the tunnel lights, but again no firm evidence, just another theory.

When Helen Newson took the stand she had a lot of questions put to her, she confirmed that Les didn't drink alcohol, let alone anything like what they were saying he did. She confirmed that he packed his own lunch, filled up his own milk bottle and went to work as normal. She then agreed that he had gone for a job as a bus driver in 1965 but had been turned down because, "he did not have enough road sense". The more they dug into his life the more it became distressing for Helen. The questions were so intense and so personal that she ended up breaking down in the witness stand. Being led away with help, she waited until she was out of the court before collapsing on the floor.

Now the inquest focused on the equipment of the train; shockingly now people were told that the train had no speedometer and had to rely on guesswork and experience. Dr Paul questioned this: "How is a motorman supposed to observe speed restrictions and the guard to know that he is observing those restrictions when there is no speedometer on 1938 stock?"

Mr Frederick Collins, an area manager for LT working from the Barbican, said that it would take possibly two to three months for a driver or guard to get the necessary experience in this "guesswork".

Now it was the turn of Dr Roy Goulding, who was called by Helen Newson for a second opinion on the alcohol level findings. He said that although he did not disagree with Dr Ann Robinson's analysis, "we may diverge on the interpretation of the meaning of them," and that he would not have been driven to the conclusion that Les had been drinking alcohol before the crash. This didn't mean he rejected the possibility of him consuming alcohol, merely that the amount consumed would only have had minimal impairment of Newson's driving ability. Because Robinson's findings were so out of character with Newson, the coroner had agreed for this second opinion to take place. Robinson herself said that there were so many unknown factors that she could not be definite about the amount of alcohol in the blood at the time of the crash. But in her opinion she had been brought to the inevitable conclusion that he had swallowed alcohol.

Dr Goulding thought the alcohol findings of Dr Robinson could have been accounted for entirely by chemical changes in the body after death. He also placed no reliance on the minute amount of alcohol found in the sour milk bottle, the amount being within the normal limits of what would be found in sour milk. Microbiologist Dr John Williams said that in order to produce alcohol after death there would have to have been sugar present.

Two new theories were brought up by expert Dr Phillip Raffles. He agreed that the blood alcohol levels wouldn't account for his actions in the seconds before the crash, even if he had consumed that much. He put forward that he could have suffered from 1) a brain haemorrhage which made him immobile or 2) transinglobal amnesia, a condition that would have left him completely unaware of what he was doing and in turn totally forgetting how to drive the train. Again there was no evidence to back this up, just another theory like the rest.

Ray Deadman took the stand to tell how he had qualified Newson in an eight-hour course and said that Newson had been so overcautious that he remembered him long after the event. Another station worker said how he would drink his tea and never smell of any kind of alcohol, even offering his milk to his workmates, this being the only liquid he drank. If any alcohol was present they would have definitely known about it.

Terry Hall's parents went to the inquest to hear how their daughter died, like so many others. They would sit and hear that their daughter died "standing up" and of asphyxiation. When they wanted to ask questions though, they were promptly dismissed.

The inquest heard the sixty-one witnesses give a total of twenty-six hours of evidence, including twelve people who were on the platform that morning watching train 272 enter Moorgate. With all the witnesses dismissed, the inquest was brought to an end on Friday 18th April, and summed up by the coroner who called the guard Robert Harris "a rather feckless and irresponsible young man".

The jury was out for just an hour and fifteen minutes before coming to the conclusion that all forty-two people including the driver had died due to accidental death. It could find no reasonable reason for the cause of the crash, but was critical of the actions of the guard in the minutes leading up to the point of impact.

*

The inquiry was completed in just over a year with a report published by Lt Col Ian McNaughton, Chief Inspectorate of Railways, on 4th June 1976. Before anybody had got to see the details the Daily Mail had already run an article that day saying that the report cited the cause as the actions of the driver Les Newson. The article openly admitted the report was secret until its release and although extensive investigations were carried out, the person who leaked it was never found. The newspaper headlines ran the story under the banner: *"Did motorman's suicide cause the great Tube disaster?"*

Once again no firm cause of the crash was pinpointed but it did say that there was nothing to suggest anything other than the actions of Newson as the cause of the disaster, but it did not say that he committed suicide. If there had been any evidence of this both the inquiry and the inquest would have picked up on it straight away. For those who had connections with the disaster, the unanswered questions would be forever up in the air.

8. Causes and Conspiracies

The decades since the crash at Moorgate have led to thousands of people voicing their own opinions based on "facts" and "inside information" that in most cases simply does not exist. In researching this book I have come across a huge number of people who had formed an opinion of the cause of the crash based on the rumours and false information that has been passed from one colleague or friend to another. But before we look at these we will take a look at Laurence Marks, son of Bernard Marks.

As a reporter for the Sunday Times, and following the loss of his father, Laurence took it upon himself in less than a week to research as much as he could about the disaster and follow the inquiries with interest. It is interesting to note that less than forty-eight hours after the crash his name appears on the front page of the Observer on 2nd March 1975 as the reporter who has written the article. For forty-eight weeks after the crash he would speak to a large number of people including the family of driver Les Newson. Whether his presence would be welcomed was a completely different matter.

He turned up at Helen Newson's home in the hope of being able to talk about her husband, as he had lost his father in the crash, deliberately leaving out the fact that he also worked for the press. The Newsons were told by Marks that he just wanted some closure and wanted to "lay a few ghosts to rest". They invited him in believing he was nothing more than a grieving relative.

Straight away he got down to the point, he put forward to her the reports that her husband had been a heavy drinker to which Helen dismissed them straight away. She went over to the tall cabinet and slid the door open for him to see. Inside was a small array of various spirits – whisky, sherry, Advocaat and Bacardi. These had been sat in this cupboard for at least three years and were reserved for guests should they want a drink. The top of the cabinet was glass for displays and inside were novelty Babycham glasses amongst the collection, coated in a thin layer of dust from the length of time they had sat there without anybody touching them. The Bacardi had been there so long that the top had started to crumble. None of the bottles had ever been opened and remained sealed, and had been since they had been bought. After a while Laurence got up and left, continuing his investigation elsewhere.

On Sunday 29th February 1976 Marks published his report in the Sunday Times. In it he claims that Helen Newson had said that the Bacardi had possibly gone down from when she had last checked, a claim which horrified Diane and Sandra. "The drink was not even opened so how could it have gone down? He was making the theories fit the evidence!"

*

In Laurence Marks' article in Woman magazine of 4th March 1978 (titled *A Train To Nowhere*) he says Professor Simpson discounted epilepsy due to there being no sign of a bitten tongue. He also says that the Coroner Dr David Paul had pulled him to one side and gave his opinion off the record that he believed it to be a case of suicide by the driver.

Marks also gives the impression that Newson was very isolated, lonely and with very few friends. The Newsons, however, give the complete opposite view – a loving family man who was always chatting, very friendly, would go on holiday to see relatives and talk openly to workmates. A man who was very popular and ex army, he was anything but a lonely man. More than 130 London Underground employees were at his funeral around three weeks after the crash, they were spilling out of the door there were that many of them! He was cremated at Lewisham Crematorium. The guard himself spoke highly of him in The Sunday Times article of 2nd March 1975 giving the following report: Asked for his impressions of Newson, Harris said that because of the differences in age, they did not take lunch together, but he had found Newson a reliable man to work with. "*He was a very straightforward fellow. If he had a bone to pick with you he would pick it, but that didn't often happen. He was a very jolly fellow who had a good sense of humour. **He was not a loner**.*"

The day after the crash, Harris had spent three hours with investigators at Euston, having to be sedated when describing the disaster as he was suffering from shock. He had only been a guard for six months and was happy with it because it was a safe and secure job. When the train arrived at Drayton Park he had said to Les, "OK Les, a few more trips and then we're off for a break," to which Les replied, "Yes mate," and the journey would commence.

Marks claims that the time Les overshot the platform slightly a few days before was a trial run for a suicide that he was planning. He would get suicide experts to agree with this scenario, likening it to taking an overdose but leaving several pills still in the bottle so it was obvious what you had done. This kind of overshoot was, however, a common occurrence in drivers at the time and it happened literally hundreds of times, but knowing Les Newson he would have reported it and owned up straight away. If you take the five stations on his line, times that by the number of journeys there and back, then times that by the number of days, you are looking at thousands of times you have to stop that train every few minutes at the exact same spot. The law of averages says that one time you will over-run and go that little bit too far, and this is what Les is most likely to have done. He would have been annoyed with himself for it, he would have deemed it unprofessional and silently cursed himself for being so lax. Just because everybody else had done it now and again doesn't mean to say he could join them, he would make sure he would try his damned hardest to make sure it wouldn't happen again.

However for people to seriously consider an overshoot to be a "trial run" for a suicide is absurd. If anybody is going to take their life they are not going to have a test first to see if they like it! If it was a trial run what was he hoping to achieve? All he did was stop the train a few feet further down than he should have done. In what way would that have convinced Les that ramming his train into a brick wall was a good idea to end it all? That theory not only makes no sense whatsoever, but if it wasn't so tragic, it would be laughable.

One issue he does keep bringing up is an issue of Les Newson being impotent. He claims that Newson had been to the doctors just two months before the crash and had been told he was impotent which would have thrown him into a spate of depression. Marks doesn't explain where he got this information from or how he was able to access his confidential medical records. It is also interesting to note that the question of his impotence was never brought up at the inquest. The fact he had two daughters and he was approaching his 60s, would this really have made a difference to his life to the point of his slamming a rush hour train into a wall and killing his passengers? The only medical condition that ever bothered him was some skin problems which caused him to itch until it bled. He also had several boils on the back of his neck which he had had since the war. He had never shown signs of diabetes and had never sat staring into space, which is why the actions of Les on the morning of the crash were so strange.

It was in 2006 that Marks was involved with a documentary team in making a film about his life. His career had been a successful one, after his journalism he went on to team up with writer Maurice Gran and pen some of the best known British sitcoms of the 20th Century, with many of his shows being household names such as *Goodnight Sweetheart, Birds of a Feather* and *Shine on Harvey Moon*. It was when this programme was in the research stage that Sandra Newson was contacted by the film company via letter for some information. The researchers then came to Diane's house to ask for a statement to be used in the documentary. The documentary was going to focus heavily on his crash theory as well as his film career so needless to say anything to do with Moorgate was important to the story. Diane and Sandra wrote one and a half pages of information for them, but they looked at it and said they couldn't put that in the filming…try condensing it…to maybe one or two lines they said! They did prepare a statement and sent it to the researcher but the quotes were never used until a brief mention at the end, the entire documentary being about Laurence himself, his father, the crash, his interpretation of the cause and then going into his writing career. It was screened on 4th June 2006 on Channel 4 to a flurry of comments online, mostly supporting Les Newson and dismissing his entire investigation.

One person who would talk openly was fireman Brian Goodfellow, who would talk about the crash on film for the first time and this became really the first time he had opened up about what he saw at Moorgate. Visibly distressed as he recounted his story on how he found "The City Gent", Lawrence showed him a photograph of his father. Brian recognised him straight away before turning away in tears.

*

Once again the debate on the cause of the disaster was reopened, but it did not come any closer to an answer. It did however reveal a surprising fact. Laurence claimed that he had stolen the inquest report after the coroner advised him that, not in so many words, he would leave it on his desk and be back later. After photocopying the document in its entirety he accidentally put the photocopy back on the coroner's desk and left with the original. He also says that after the inquest had finished the coroner had, again not in so many words, believed it to be suicide but there was just a lack of official evidence. What is on official record though, and in all the newspapers, is that Dr David Paul, City of London Coroner, said the suggestion of suicide is "completely bizarre and without foundation." Did he say that to the press just because he was obliged to, or did he seriously believe his own words? Laurence Marks says differently.

*

Now it comes to my research into Moorgate for this book. As I was interviewing a lot of different people it became apparent that 99% of them had very different opinions and that the amount of speculation had led to such confusion that they had completely forgotten about what the inquiry and inquests had said. Dave Bolton worked for London Underground and said to me that sometimes back in the day drivers would swap halfway through a shift which was not allowed. There were no drink-drive rules like today and some drivers would go to the pub for lunch and a pint. This was more common than was first thought, but it wasn't illegal, in fact it wasn't even frowned upon. The drivers were safe enough and they wouldn't come to work drunk as they would instantly lose their jobs. However, this didn't apply to Les Newson…Dave knew Les and he knew he wasn't a drinker.

Another family of one of the victims met with me and told me what they had heard over the years. Lots of people who knew Les said he was "a known drunk, a known depressive – always up and down" and the best one was the "fact" that Les used to bring beer to work to drink with his lunch! Another said that he was always drinking and on the day of the crash he fell asleep on the job and crashed the train. Another in the same family said that they had heard the train was defective. The guard was setting up the train for the return journey before it had even finished this trip and that was why he wasn't at his post.

Motorman John Baldwin had also heard that there were rumours of mechanical faults and instantly his mind went back to when he did that journey before Les took over. "That could so easily have been me," he began to think.

A meeting of the Forensic Science Society was called and this took place in the McMorran Hall at Wood Street Police Station. (The Hall has since been renamed the C H Rolph Hall, after a well known ex-City Police journalist and broadcaster.) The members of the FSS were concerned that this meeting should not be reported in the press. The Chairman, a medical doctor, asked anyone present (of about 150) to declare if they had a press interest, stating that it was a condition of attendance that nothing should be reported. It was agreed. The meeting was to discuss the effects of the lighting in the tunnel (as to whether it was thought the intermittent flashing of these lights mesmerised the train driver as he passed them). Could it have been a bizarre suicide? Also the agenda was to include whether alcohol could be developed in a dead body after death – this was critical to the post mortem findings. A lady pathologist was invited to speak on this subject and the meeting duly took place in this secure hall.

*

So let's have a closer look at the life of the driver behind the Moorgate crash. Leslie Benjamin Newson was born on 30th August 1919 and when war broke out he was thrust into military life at just twenty years old. Working on one of the huge guns during the war, he became suddenly and seriously injured. His job there was as a gun loader, when one of the shells misfired and shot out backwards, plunging into his stomach and leaving him in agony. He was immediately sent to hospital and he remained in a serious condition for several months. It would be a total of six months before he was fit for duty and went back out to serve his country again. In 1940 came the terrifying news that thousands of British troops were trapped at Dunkirk, literally just across the Channel from freedom. Hitler's war machine had pushed them as far back as they could go. If a miracle didn't happen soon then there would be a massacre.

But a miracle did happen. Hundreds of Brits heard the news about their soldiers being stuck in France and they put to sea in every kind of boat possible. Pleasure craft, motor launches, yachts – anything with an engine attached – were put to sea to help with the rescue. In what became known as the "miracle of Dunkirk" tens of thousands of soldiers were plucked from the beaches of Dunkirk to be taken back to their homeland safe from the advancing German army. One of these rescued soldiers was Les Newson. He would never speak about his experiences at Dunkirk, except to remark to a friend at work about the time he was sharing a tent with members of his platoon there – probably trying to put him off going on a camping holiday! Although he took part in many campaigns, Les would never like to talk about the war. He said it was in the past and that's where it was going to stay. He was, however, decorated on more than one occasion, receiving the Africa Star (1940-43), Italy Star (1943-45) and the War Medal (1939-1945).

His time in the war had not just left his body a wreck but it had had a permanent effect on his hearing. The noise of the guns going off had perforated an eardrum and he was deaf in one ear. His family would say, "If you talked to him on the wrong side he'd just go 'What?' and if he didn't want to listen to you he would lay on his good ear."

Despite the injuries received in the Second World War, Les Newson was fit for his age. At the time of the crash he was fifty-five years old and loved his life. He enjoyed working for London Transport, loved his family and loved his food, especially cakes and puddings! He always had a sweet tooth and would have three heaped spoonfuls of sugar in his tea, having several cups at a time too! Despite this he never had a history of diabetes and certainly wasn't overweight!

So now let's take a look at the drinking habits of this man. Well basically, he didn't have one! Despite the decades of rumours and false reports, Les Newson was virtually teetotal. The only time alcohol ever touched his lips was when he would force himself to have half a glass of brown ale at Christmastime and he would even struggle to drink that. Everybody in his family knew that he didn't like it and that the only reason he would be sat there with an ale was because all the relatives gathered around were drinking and he felt out of place. Sandra once said to him, "Why do you drink it dad? You blatantly don't like it!" to which he just replied, "Ah it's Christmas, you have to have a drink." He would only manage half a pint as he couldn't stomach any more. "He would drink it like it was poison," said Sandra. After his annual half an ale he would be back to his soft drinks for the rest of the night.

Even on special occasions he wouldn't drink and he certainly didn't go out to the pub with his friends. He would pride himself on being a family man and would go straight home after work and plan with Helen what to do on the upcoming weekends, usually involving going down the coast.

Another story to hit the press, which must have been agony for the Newsons, was that the medical records had somehow been accessed and it was printed that Les suffered from erectile problems. This fuelled the suicide theory for their story although it was a weak excuse at best. In addition, the local landlords of the nearby pubs jumped on the bandwagon and told the papers how Les was always in their pub and was regarded as one of the regulars.

The truth is that Helen wore the trousers in the Newson house, so if Les had been down to the pub for just one pint she would have been able to tell and he wouldn't have heard the last of it! Her dad was a heavy drinker who spent his wages on booze instead of food for the family and for that reason she would never have tolerated any misuse of alcohol; she had seen first hand what it had done to her family. She didn't like going down to the pub herself and Les didn't drink, and for Les to have had this secret private life that Helen didn't know about was completely out of the question. He ran his day like clockwork, he would arrive home at certain times of the day after coming straight back after the finish of his shift. In Les's own words, "I don't drink, it's a waste of money to piss it up the wall. I have to work really hard for this money I'm not going to waste it."

Finally just to cover one last hurdle, an article in the Daily Mail stated: *Dr Ann Robinson, senior lecturer in forensic medicine at the London Hospital Medical College, examined a sample of Mr Newson's blood. Says the inspector: "She concluded that Newson had drunk alcohol on the morning of his death, but that the highest possible level of alcohol in the blood at the time of the post-mortem was about 80 milligrams per 100 millilitres. I have subsequently been advised... that it is generally accepted that as much as 80 milligrams of alcohol may make its appearance as a result of the growth of micro-organisms and fungi in a decomposing body."*

One other point on the alcohol in the body of Les Newson comes in the format of Laurence Marks' newspaper article. He says that alcohol can be produced naturally by the body if: *"yeast is present (which it was not) and in conditions conducive to growth, which means that sugar must be present as well (it was not)."* That was in Mark's own words published in a letter to the Sunday Times dated 14th March 1976.

I can now reveal that sugar WAS present in the body of Leslie Newson, a large quantity at that! A small but very relevant fact was obtained by me, which had been overlooked for almost forty years, when I interviewed the Newsons. I asked them what kind of a man Les was...who was he...what did he like to do...what were his interests? I wanted to know the man behind the photo.

Ah yes, the photo, that famous photo of Les that graced the pages of the newspapers just hours after the crash. That is another story! On the day of the crash a man appeared at the door of their home and put his foot in the door to prevent it closing, insisting he was an official who needed a photograph of Les for identification purposes. This was no more than two hours after the crash. Sandra hadn't even arrived there yet, so Helen grabbed a passport photo of her husband and handed it over. Overcome with worry and hoping that she had done the right thing, she didn't realise that she had just been duped by a despicable news reporter. The photo was in every newspaper by the following morning. Straight away the family took legal action and he faced a serious charge, but this all fell through when he walked free without so much as a caution. The Newson family never got the photograph back and that is now out of their hands in the public domain. (I have purposely left this photograph out of this book and instead show the reader more human images of Les direct from the Newson family album.)

So the Newsons began chatting to me about his various characteristics, his war record, his medical issues and his social life. A random comment about his choice of beverage was the clincher that didn't hit me until over a year later; not the alcohol that everybody seems to cling to, but none other than a good old cup of tea. Les always had time for a brew, several cups at a time in fact. And in each of his cups of tea he would put three heaped spoonfuls of sugar. He had always had a vast amount of sugar, taking two cups of tea every time the kettle boiled. On the morning of the crash he had two cups before he went to work, and at least one other cup before starting his shift, each with three sugars in. This made a total of nine to twelve heaped spoonfuls of sugar in just a few hours, which again was normal for Les, but a fact that had not been known for the simple reason the right questions had never been asked. This would account for a slightly higher alcohol reading in Les's blood than the other eight bodies examined nearby. Add to that the fact that he was in his own cab at the very top of the tunnel wall (heat rises remember!) and you have a higher temperature in a more confined space with a hell of a lot of sugar; add the heat factor of four days at 100 degrees and you have a teetotal man who has now the blood of a heavy drinker.

*

Now looking at the theory of Les Newson committing suicide. Again you have to look at the original inquest and inquiry that clearly stated that, although they cannot say for definite it didn't happen, they can also find no evidence to say otherwise. The cause of the crash was entirely the fault of Les, there is no question about that. But let's examine the arguments for his ending his life first.

Now to start with a suicidal man like Les has to have a *reason* to kill himself. He enjoyed life, loved his job, was always immaculately dressed and was overjoyed to have his 7-month-old grandson Robert in his life. He was planning to go back to Canada to visit his brother and was even talking of emigrating. In his bag was £273 of Diane's money to buy her car when he finished his shift (it was falsely reported in the press that this was a present for her birthday – her birthday had already come and gone the previous month). He had assured her that he would look after her money in his bag and have it with him the whole day. He had planned his day and knew what he wanted to do when he got back home. (She didn't end up buying the car in question, instead purchasing a Ford Escort that leaked anyway.)

Another aspect of the suicide theory that people are failing to take into account is the fact he took forty-two of his passengers with him. Would a man who saved lives in the army during the war and fought for the freedom of his country then end it all by speeding into an end tunnel knowing full well that everybody who was directly behind him would die? Les was a caring man, comforting Sandra one day when she had witnessed a man opening fire with a shotgun in the middle of a London street and killing his girlfriend. He was always there for anybody who needed help and wouldn't hurt a fly. He had plans for the rest of his life: trips abroad, visiting family, watching his grandson grow up and enjoying the fruits of his labour. He was not the sort of person who would sink into old age and let his life collapse around him. So why all of a sudden would he turn from the kindest man in the world to a mass killer? Well it's simple…he didn't. Again there is no evidence to even suggest that he was suicidal, especially from those close to him who would have picked up on any change straightaway.

*

Now we will examine the technical aspects of the train in relation to the disaster. The master controller, also known as the "dead man's handle", is the fail safe of any train of the modern age. Should pressure be released from this then the train's brakes are automatically applied and, until physically worked on by recharging the brakes and altering a host of keys, levers and switches, the train cannot move an inch. One other theory at the time is that the dead man's handle was neutralised while still in use by Les. This is achieved by placing the handle into the 3 o'clock position, at which point the reverser key can be moved from "forward" to "off" deactivating the handle, this is called "centering" the key. Now you could simply let go of the handle and the train would carry on as normal with minimum effort from the motorman. This is the train equivalent of putting a car into neutral gear while it is still driving forward. It would neither speed up nor slow down, but if a driver were to do this and suffer some kind of problem (for example a heart attack) then the safe train would then be a runaway train. An obvious safety nightmare should a driver do this, not to mention it being blatant negligence in deactivating a safety device, the papers were the first to suspect that this had been the cause of the crash. Les had simply been lazy and wanted to relax a bit more before having some kind of attack and collapsing at the controls, leaving the train driverless and speeding off into the inevitable.

However, this theory was immediately shot down on discovery that the master controller was still in the "Series" position (half power) and the reverser key was in "Forward 1" position. This was a slower rate of acceleration away from Old Street and therefore a slightly slower impact speed at Moorgate. This proves that Les didn't intend crashing the train deliberately as he focused on a steady speed instead of going hell-bent into the wall at maximum. This also shows that whatever happened to him happened just seconds after departure from Old Street, he didn't have chance to put the train into full power to make the journey at the usual speed and arrive on time. Although saying that, he was known to be "overcautious" by Ray Deadman and had a reputation for gliding into stations slower than any other driver. This was his own habit which in some cases cost him time on the runs, sometimes only by thirty seconds to a minute but still later than others.

*

This now leads me on to the real cause of the Moorgate disaster, which doesn't start on the day of the crash it actually starts several months earlier, on 21st June 1974. Les Newson was at work doing his normal shift and was walking along the platform at one of the stations when he came upon a man attacking a woman in one of his carriages. As he went to help her, the man suddenly turned on him and hit Les several times around the head. The man was arrested and the woman was saved from further harm, but Les had received cuts and bruises to the right side of his head and face. He was sent to the hospital later for checks and given the all clear – because he wasn't unconscious this wasn't deemed an emergency or of any real concern. It is shocking to note that the previous year there had been 850 assaults on bus staff and 175 on London Underground staff by members of the public, according to the *Railway Review* of 7th June 1974 when they published the figures.

So now we can fast-forward nearly four decades and we have a reason to reinvestigate this attack. At the time of the disaster it was said that heart attack was ruled out, as was epilepsy. Now a heart attack could be detected post mortem, but new information on the brain has led me to go back down the epilepsy route and look at the advances in medical knowledge that have been made since the 1970s. With a blow to the head it is entirely possible that Les had received more damage to his brain than first suspected. If you remember his war record, he was injured severely due to a shell misfire and he was deaf in one ear. Add this together with his attack and you have a catalogue of injuries that today would leave you off work and possibly on a permanent disability pension. This is where my focus lay and I began to make enquiries.

After speaking to several experts in epilepsy I learned that there are forty different types of epilepsy, of which several conditions would leave the body separate from the brain in the fact that it would carry on as normal but the brain would have literally switched off like a light. This kind of blackout would leave Les sat bolt upright and staring straight ahead, the pressure would have been kept on the dead man's handle and as the train slammed into the tunnel wall he didn't even put his hands up to shield his face – raising your hands is a normal reaction for anybody about to hit something head on even if you know you are about to die; it is human instinct. The truth of the matter is that as the train left Old Street it was just seconds before Les's brain would switch off. These seizures only last a few minutes at most, but as the train picked up speed naturally on its journey, it was too late to stop unless he snapped out of it. There was nothing anybody could do to shake him out of it. If he had had the seizure at any other station he could have woken up with a jolt and sought medical attention, either way he may have refused to drive the train any further until he was sure he was medically fit. The fact that this occurred at a dead end tunnel which had been widened for national trains was simply a case of bad luck. There was only one thing that could have stopped the disaster: after a previous train collision a lot of terminal stations were fitted with a device on the tracks that automatically applies the brakes if the train is coming in too fast. At Moorgate station, this was not fitted.

The SUDEP (Sudden Death by Epilepsy) organisation's *Headway* fact sheet describes an epileptic seizure as follows: "An epileptic seizure is a sudden change in movement, behaviour or perception caused by uncontrolled electrical activity in the brain."

During a seizure, the nerve cells in the brain become overactive and fire off in a random and erratic fashion. This activity often disturbs neighbouring cells which can also become overactive and set up a kind of "chain reaction" so that an area of the brain or the whole brain can become temporarily upset. Sometimes this over-activity can occur with no obvious external evidence, but commonly the person shows signs and symptoms such as change in or loss of consciousness, shaking or convulsing, tongue biting etc.

Generalised tonic-clonic seizures, sometimes referred to as "grand mal" seizures, are characterised by sudden loss of consciousness and falling, followed by stiffening (tonic phase) and then rhythmic jerking of the whole body (clonic phase). The person may bite their tongue or lips, or be incontinent. Following this there may be a period of drowsiness, confusion or sleep. Generalised tonic-clonic seizures are sometimes preceded by a strange taste, smell or other sensation, known as an "aura" which tends to occur in the same way before each seizure.

Next you have partial seizures – sometimes referred to as "petit-mal" seizures (although this term is falling out of use). These affect only part of the brain. Changes in consciousness and behaviour occur, such as lip-smacking, picking at clothing, grimacing and unresponsiveness. These seizures can also have symptoms of sudden anger, panic, depression and other states of mind.

The Epilepsy Society gives a rundown of the different types of seizures. It says that "dissociative seizures" (DS) are often caused by traumatic events such as:
- An accident
- Severe emotional upset (such as the death of a loved one)
- Psychological stress (such as a divorce)
- Difficult relationships
- Physical or sexual abuse
- Being bullied

It can be hard to find the cause of someone's DS. For some, they start shortly after a specific event. For others, they may not start until years later or they may start suddenly for no apparent reason. Once DS have started, they might be triggered or brought on when the person is stressed or frightened. Or they might happen spontaneously in situations that are not stressful or frightening."

*

As for the brakes on the train itself, anybody could have opened the Drivers Brake Isolating Valve while approaching the station, the effect would have given an audible warning to the driver in his cab and the train would have continued on with noise in his ear. Opening the valve would slam the brakes on and the only way to take off the brakes was to recharge the air in the pipes. These brakes work the opposite way to how a car works. If you cut the brake pipes on a car the hydraulic fluid leaks out and the brakes don't work. If a leak develops on a train's brakes then it causes the train to stop, it takes pressure in the system to force the brakes to release the wheels and allow movement. These were the first trains to have control circuits, everything being 650 volts including the master controller. A triple valve would allow you to put air into the cylinder to release the brakes when you reduce the train line air. If there is no air in the cylinders then the train simply won't move. This puts to rest the conspiracy theory of the brakes being faulty. If they had been faulty then the train would never have been able to move an inch.

Terence Lowe from the Department of Mechanical Engineering at LT told the Evening Standard on 14th March 1975 that one car had had its brakes isolated (in other words, it had no brakes that day), but stronger braking on the other five cars would have automatically compensated for this. All braking equipment was in satisfactory condition on each car. The position of the camshaft indicated that the train had been motoring to within two seconds of impact.

*

David Henderson, a London bus driver contacted me in 2014 to explain an incident that had occurred to him in the late 1990s that showed just how a medical condition can suddenly appear. Working for First Northampton he was in his late twenties and was a reasonably healthy man, not a drinker or a heavy smoker. He went to see a doctor as he was unusually tired all the time and would fall asleep anywhere, to which the doctor suggested he get some exercise and go to bed earlier. So one day not long after this he was at work driving his bus which was full of people on an early shift across the town. He yawned and stopped at the traffic lights to wait for the green signal. With a jolt he felt people start to get off the bus, but he was no longer at the traffic lights. He had fallen asleep, driven the bus 600 yards from the lights, over another set of lights, round two right turns and a sharp left and stopped at the correct stop. Although he was quite some way from the kerb he was shocked that all this had happened subconsciously right into the bus station. Scared out of his wits he got off the bus and was immediately booked off work sick. It turned out he had Chronic Obstructive Sleep Apnoea (OSA), caused by the shape of his jaw being set back. When he fell asleep it was found that he would completely stop breathing, during one observation he did this 411 times in one night. Although this was the '90s, this type of phenomenon was very rarely known about, especially, when being fast asleep he was able to drive the bus as if he was completely conscious. Although this is not thought to be anything to do with the cause of the Moorgate crash, I have used this example as something the reader can digest and then realise that conditions like this do exist and many of them are not known about to the general public unless you do a lot of research into that particular one. For David Henderson, he was lucky that he was sensible enough to not simply go about his business and get back behind the wheel, if it had happened again he might not have been so lucky.

*

The family of David Wilson said this about the cause of the crash: "To our minds, in truth, no really convincing explanation has been offered as to the cause of the accident. For certain, trip equipment on the brakes of trains entering the station would have prevented the accident, as now applies, and other technical issues such as the size of the carriages, perhaps also. All manner of accusations were made regarding the driver such as him being suicidal, alcoholic (the press made much of alcohol having being identified in his body until it was pointed out that fermentation processes within a body will inevitably produce alcohol over time, not least after three days in a hot tunnel) etc., but no real evidence has appeared to confirm or dispute these theories and all this innuendo can only have distressed his own family who, no less than us, had lost a dear family member. Perhaps we will never know. David was a wonderful young man and our beloved brother and the son our Mum and Dad always wanted. He was a typical teenager, loving, considerate and always to be relied upon. Up to the moment of the accident he had a great future ahead of him."

*

Although some of the technical aspects may be a bit foreign to the reader (as to myself while researching this) I have put this into the best terms that I can in order to explain why the train was not the cause of the crash, not simply saying that as fact but telling each part individually in order to show the layman how the 1938 stock worked. The Marks investigation, in the words of the Newson family, was based on getting the theories to fit the evidence. Whenever a police officer is personally involved in any investigation, such as family members being in an accident or a relative committing a crime, that officer is immediately taken off the investigation due to a conflict of interest. An investigation can be highly prejudiced and go in entirely the wrong direction due to the emotional state of involvement and the high desire to find a quick answer. I personally do not blame Marks for what he did, but the hurt caused to others due to his newspaper and TV reports was crossing a line. The newspapers in question should have taken him away from the investigation the second it was known that his father had been on the train. This would have saved four decades of heartache and not knowing the truth for many people.

I am pleased that I re-investigated this crash, a lot of family members and survivors wanted real questions answered that the police could not answer at the time. Not being connected to this disaster at all allowed me the blank sheet I could start on with a completely open mind. After over four years of interviews and trips to archives, libraries and most of all random places in London, I believe my conclusions and evidence are the best that there are going to be. After reviewing all the information available and seeing a lot of items and stores that were "off the record", a sudden epileptic seizure caused by previous head injury is the reason Les Newson did not slow his train down on the morning of 28th February 1975.

As much as the conspiracy clubs would rather it was more than that, I am sorry to burst your bubble. The truth is far simpler, leaving nobody to blame, unless you count the man who attacked Les on the tube eight months previously. This man I cannot name because I simply don't have it, he has obviously served what little sentence he would have got for assaulting Les. The woman who Les went to assist was named in the Daily Mirror just over two weeks after the crash as 18-year-old Debbie Connolly. The headline of that edition simply said: "*My Hero.*"

For Helen Newson she would never get the peace that most of the victims had. She would often go into a trance and have to be shaken out of it by her daughters, she would then say, "You should have left me I was OK." She had a host of disturbing letters sent to the family including one with a picture of a coffin drawn on it demanding money. On top of this she was asked by probate if Les had any illegitimate children, at which point she broke down in pieces. In 1976 the Newsons had the opportunity to speak on TV with a documentary crew in which she reiterated her belief that her husband was not to blame for the crash. Her comments were welcomed by most people who trusted in her husband, but this was of little comfort in the end. Helen McEwen Forsyth Newson died of emphysema on 14th September 2002 at the age of seventy-nine. She was cremated at West Herts Crematorium in Garston nine days later.

9. Aftermath of a tragedy

After Jeff Benton's incredible but tragic fight for life in hospital, it was obvious that burying him wouldn't be enough for his wife Val. She started to raise money in his memory; on one occasion she persuaded her work to do a disco one evening at the local sports club in Winchmore Hill, which went off well. A man who attended this saw Keith Benton in the toilets and started speaking to him, he had known Jeff and remarked that it was very strange talking to him as he looked the spitting image of his brother. The money raised that night was a decent amount which was given to the London Hospital. They used it to buy an additional dialysis unit which was placed in a small room dedicated to Jeff's memory, which would be used as a "rescue room" for equipment storage in case of another major incident. A plaque on the door was unveiled to commemorate the event.

After attending every day at the inquest for two weeks, Val would head out of the UK to South Africa to start a new life around two years after the crash. At the time she worked for a travel agent so was able to get reduced price travel, and started a new life abroad, going into property developing when she eventually settled there. Although she remarried in the coming years and had two daughters, she never lost touch with Jeff's family and always made time to visit his parents.

It was unfortunate and with sadness that Jeff was victim number forty-two. On 10th June 1975 the Moorgate disaster would take a forty-third and final victim when 23-year-old Jane Simpson died in St Bart's Hospital. The sides of the train seat had ruptured her kidneys and she had suffered major injury in that area. In her months in hospital she was awake in her bed and had even met Prince Charles in the days following the crash. As her death came after the official inquests she was not officially counted amongst the Moorgate victims in that case and would have to be dealt with separately. Her passing would receive only a small piece in the national newspapers.

*

The official Moorgate Disaster Fund was set up for donations to be given to help the grieving families with any undue expenses caused by the sudden loss of their loved one. This could help with bills, funeral expenses, travel costs etc. Money became a headline once again when on 25th November

1975 the papers reported that the parents of Janet Cook had been offered just £500 compensation by London Transport with an additional £350 loss of earnings and £143 towards the funeral costs. She had been cremated after several days missing in the wreckage with many people turning up to say their farewells, however, the family were still very traumatised and the talk of money was not the important issue in these early days of grieving. This highlighted in the press the fact that people were accepting small amounts of compensation when they were not in their right minds, being still overwhelmed by grief even nine months on. London Transport was insured for major incidents and it was estimated that claims could run up to £1million, however, the Payne family were offered just £700, where Teresa Eva, wife of victim Sidney Eva, received her offer of £4700 which she took straight away after advice from her solicitor. She was so upset she didn't fight for any more.

It was because of the disaster that two families would be united as good friends for life. It was a few days after the crash, on Tuesday 4th March, that Stephen Payne's parents Sheila and Ken saw the story of Janice Donovan in the newspaper and, together with Ken's brother Ray, decided to go round to introduce themselves as they had a unique but tragic connection and literally only lived round the corner. After meeting and discussing the sad chain of events that led them to this point, they have been very close friends ever since. The Donovans told how the first compensation offer from London Underground was just £750 because they had not lost anything "monetarily". This comment alone left them shocked and, after rejecting the initial offer, they ended up getting just over £1000, a small price for the life of a loved one.

Stephen's funeral took place on Thursday 6th March at St Edmonds at Chingford. A memorial tree with a stone vase bearing his name rests in Enfield Crematorium. Well-wishers and ex-work colleagues, even old school teachers and childhood friends, would send cards and letters to the Payne family for their loss. They even received condolences from people whom they didn't even know. The headmaster of his old school sent a very nice letter which said simply: "So many children pass through the school as the years go by that often faces and names become blurred, but Stephen is one of those boys whose friendly and cheerful disposition is readily recalled. We shall long remember him."

Janice Donovan's funeral took place the day after on Friday 7th March at St John's Church on Chingford Road, the same place where she was due to be married in the May. Her body was interred in Queens Road Cemetery in Walthamstow under a barrage of flowers and well-wishers.

The family of 17-year-old David Wilson had a very sad service at Islington Crematorium, his ashes being interred in the grounds, only recently being marked by a standard rose tree. The ashes of his mother Joyce would join him years later. David's parents had separated not long before the accident so the family all carried their grief separately, Joyce having the support of her three daughters and their families. Again London Transport gave his family a derisory sum of money which was a basic amount required by regulation for the loss of a family member who was not directly considered a wage earner. His family would tell the author for this book, "In reality who among us knows what financial help David may have been to his mother in the ensuing years?"

On 11th March the funeral of Rosemary Mansi was officiated by Cardinal John Heenan, the Archbishop of Westminster. She is buried with over half a dozen other Moorgate victims in Islington Cemetery.

*

Janet King had gone to the LT office to collect the belongings of her fiancé Peter Bradbury, the man there opening his briefcase to verify that they were Peter's, and the first thing they saw was one of his textbooks that he was using for his actuarial studies called *Life and other contingencies*. They looked at each other and realised it was a very strange and poignant moment. She gathered the items together and left the building. Not long after this she had a visit from a clergyman from Islington. "He gave me a notice declaring that the disaster had happened because the people of Islington had not been to church…what a dumbass! I'll never forget that."

Because she was in the middle of a teacher training program at King's College, the landlady very generously let her stay in the flat until the end of her course as she had nowhere to go and now very little money. Janet was suffering really badly from the loss of her Peter, luckily she had some good friends to rely on, but she needed to get away from the country for a while and so decided to go off and travel for a year, working her way around Australia and New Zealand. "I dread to think how I'd have ended up if I'd stayed." She eventually met somebody and was married in 1979, moving to the USA four years later where she lives today. Her life had a further tragic twist when she became a widow in 2005. Despite the tragedies in her life she has never stopped living her life to the full and today is a keen lover of the outdoors.

*

Fred Wonderling's funeral was held at Finchley Crematorium, his ashes are buried in East Finchley Cemetery with his mother and brother.

For the family of Antony Byczkowski, they had heard about the crash on the news on Radio 3 in the evening. They couldn't settle until they had the news that he was alright. His half brother Ronald Chapman had taken a phone call earlier on saying that Tony hadn't come home from work as he usually got the bus. Antony had been like clockwork, usually arriving home at around three minutes to 6pm so he could catch the evening news. Maybe he had gone to see friends? Not in his suit he wouldn't have, thought his mother. His sister Annette was thinking of the last time she had seen him – it had been the night before – and how she had heard the news of the crash and instantly thought he would be on it but that he would be OK. June, his elder sister by five years, rang the emergency line to see if they could get any information. Like many other families it was a case of waiting, but when it was confirmed that he was one of those killed in the crash the awful reality hit home. It wasn't until Tuesday 4th March that his body was recovered – which just happened to be Annette's thirteenth birthday. June's husband went to identify his body and confirm that it was him. His few possessions that were with him were handed over to him – blood-stained money and a steel comb bent at an angle. He was now holding all that he had to remember him by. Antony's work colleague James Bowyer went to his funeral and paid his respects, noticing a huge football wreath in Tottenham's colours (white and blue) dominating the tributes before he was cremated and taken by his mother to her home in Finchley.

It would be a long time before his sisters Margarita and Annette would go back to school, as they wanted to stay at home with their mother, the early departure of their brother coming as such a shock to them that they wanted to just be there for each other. They started having private tuition with another young girl whose father had been killed in an unrelated incident involving a crane and this went on for quite a while. Their half brother Ron would end up working for London Underground and at one point worked at Moorgate station.

Somebody else who had already begun working for London

Underground was Tony Hall, who had lost his sister Terry. He joined the company in January 1971 as a direct recruit guard, and he held this position until mid 1974 when he passed his motorman's exam. He was twenty-three at the time of the crash and working on the Piccadilly Line, so the crash gave him more than a keen interest after the loss of his sister. Over the years the Hall family had heard many different conspiracies and didn't know what to believe in the end. They even heard that the guard was setting up the train ready for the return journey before it had even got into the station. People were telling them that Les Newson was a known drunk, a depressive and always "up and down". When some of them had tried to ask questions about Moorgate they felt that London Transport were very obstructive. This fuelled belief that there was more to the stories than just rumours. But it would be thirty years after Moorgate that the family would be struck by another London Underground disaster. Terry's other sister Tina has an autistic son called James and on 7th July 2005 he was at Edgware Road station when one of four terrorist bombs was detonated. In a day that would shake the entire country, three tube trains and a bus were blown up by suicide bombers, chaos reigned in London as news crews flocked to the scene, hundreds of people being carried out alive but severely injured. Dozens were dead. James was right in the centre of it and he was always told by his family that if he was ever involved in an emergency to seek somebody out immediately. He approached a policewoman named Caroline and said, "I'm autistic, can somebody help me please?" She led him away safely and called his family for them to come and collect him. After the events of Moorgate, the entire Hall family took a vow to ring home straight away if there was ever a major incident in London. Luckily, this time it was a happier ending for the Hall family. Not so happy for many others. The bombing cost the lives of fifty-two innocent travellers and injured around 700 more.

 The aftermath of the Moorgate crash for the Hall family was the burial of Terry in Manor Park Cemetery in London; soon after that her mother developed asthma, a problem that she hadn't had since she was a child. She took herself to bed soon after Terry's death and didn't seem to get up for several months. She was in a long period of mourning for her daughter and in the end it was the family being stern with her that forced her to get out of bed and continue with her life.

 Terry's mother died on 6th August 2012, she was cremated and her ashes were buried with her Terry. The Hall family is quite a large family and very close knit, but they had very few things to remember Terry by, the few items that were found on her that day being distributed evenly. Frances kept her lighter, her mum got her watch and Christine kept her St Christopher. It was Tony who would use his influence in London Underground to remember his sister later on, which we will cover in the last chapter.

*

For 5-year-old George Mackmurdie his day at school on 28th February 1975 is now etched into his mind for life. It was just a normal day when in the early afternoon a teacher came into his class and said that they needed to take George out of the lesson and he was to go to the headmaster's office. Not understanding what was going on, he most likely thought he was in trouble for something. When he arrived he saw his father's sister there and she looked upset, saying that she had come to collect him. Why was she upset…they were due to go to a wedding in Leeds this weekend, maybe they were going to travel up north earlier than expected? In that case surely it was good news? This was confusing!

When he arrived at his home in Wood Green it seemed that the entire family had descended on his home. His granddad was drinking, his Nan was fussing over him making sure he was OK, his mother and auntie were there. But his two uncles were elsewhere, heading ten miles down the road towards the City of London and Moorgate.

They seemed to be glued to the new colour television which was showing images of a train. He didn't understand what was going on but it was obviously important. He had no idea why he had been brought out of school and was even more confused at the fact he was sat watching a drawing of a train on TV in what looked like a concertinaed set of carriages in a tunnel.

It was 10pm that night that a call came through to say that George's dad, also called George, had been on the train and had not survived. Although he doesn't remember hearing the news or recall how he was told, the image that stays with him today is that of his grandfather slamming his head against a wall and "going ballistic", with his Nan trying to calm him down but to no avail.

The days following the disaster were a blur, he was kept in the dark about a lot of things because he was still only a small child. Needless to say the trip to Leeds for the wedding was cancelled. He doesn't even remember his father's funeral, his body being laid to rest in a grave in New Southgate Cemetery. As George got older he found that he wanted to know more about his father and the crash. At the time he was not affected by his death and never knew what was going on. He does remember his mother taking them away to Spain with his sisters and their daughters. He tries hard to remember him but has no recollection of him whatsoever. He would return to his old school to try to jog his memory, but nothing. "My memories begin from that day, I remember nothing before," he would say. He even started going through a phase of wondering if he really was dead, even following somebody to a tube station thinking it was him. It seemed that George's grieving had only started years later and had hit him as fresh today as it had the other families back in 1975. What was worse for him was the fact that nobody spoke about it, nobody had any information, everybody was shielding each other from details, and the few facts that he had turned out to be not facts at all. What had really happened at Moorgate that led to his father's death and his entire family breaking down in the space of one day?

*

Thomas Thrower's funeral was conducted at Trent Park in North London. The hearse came down the road and as they turned a corner near the Arsenal stadium, a police officer wearing white gloves saluted the coffin as it went past, being followed by nine cars for family and several private cars. It was a very touching scene and his son Ken still remembers it to this day. He was buried at Trent Park, right next to Cockfosters station at the end of the Piccadilly Line, in a cemetery with no raised headstones but instead a flat grassy land full of brass plaques. In very peaceful surroundings, there is a memorial book in the chapel with a racing horse motif put in for him by Ken and his brother.

For the Thrower family they had lost a father and grandfather, a husband and a friend, a hard worker and a gentleman. It was a meeting in London with another man that would leave a bit of mystery for Ken though. Jerry Sherrick was a cab driver like Ken and he worked in Leighton, often delving into the supernatural by holding a séance and in between all that used to write poetry, reciting it on TV. One day Ken bumped into him and said hello.

"Do you want to hear one of my poems?" said Jerry.

"Oh it's Jerry Sherrick!" said Ken astonished at who he was seeing.

"Yeah!" And he started to recite one of his poems, immediately realising that it was as if he was talking to everybody about his father.

"I think we were meant to meet," said Jerry

He told Ken about a séance he had undertaken recently. "We got through to two people on that train. One was the driver. One was a passenger. The driver came through and said, "There's people on the line that shouldn't be there," and he believed it may have something to do with the plague victims being buried there and ghosts standing on the platform. He then said about the passenger. He mentioned names that were associated with Ken's family and never really paid much attention to it as they could have been any names. He talked about a little girl who used to sit between his legs and he used to brush her hair (Ken's daughter Claire). Then he went on to say, "Did your father have any problems with his lungs?" This turned out to be true because he was in St Bart's Hospital for two to three weeks not long before the accident as he had haemorrhaged at work as he had something wrong with the base of his lung.

"Yes he was in hospital as he had a problem with one of his lungs," he told him.

"Did your father ever visit an island regularly…like the Isle of Wight?"

"No, can't think of any," but by this stage it had really got to him and it had "knocked him for six". He was at Kings Cross station and he decided to go home. Only when he was driving home did he realise he used to go to Canvey Island near Southend to visit Peter (Ken's brother) every week or so. He ran into Jerry again a few weeks later and said to him, "That thing about the island was right on the mark," and he told him all about it. Jerry said to him that if he wanted to come along to another séance then he would be very welcome. He spoke with his wife about it but she persuaded him not to as it might have been too much for him; she would have been worried about his emotional wellbeing at this time. Ken's interpretation of this connection with the driver and his view was that he may have been going through a ghost station that he had already passed through. (Ghost stations are disused or half-built stations that have long closed down, but my research shows that there are no ghost stations on that line.) Jerry said that his dad was unhappy about going back home as a spirit but has no idea why.

Thomas Thrower's wife Frances never got over her husband's death. She would speak on her own as if he was still in the room. It didn't help that she was in a serious car accident on Canvey Island just after Moorgate, the whole family being trapped in the upturned car. Thankfully they all managed to get out, but not before the fire brigade had arrived and righted the car first. She lost her hearing because of it and the side of her face had gone black.

Ken had attended the inquest into the Moorgate disaster every day. He listened and took in what they had to say. Even though he found it very distressing he felt he had to go there. He noticed a man was there who had eight kids, but he felt like he made a bit of a bad comment when remarking about the loss of his daughter but still had his seven kids to keep him going.

Claire Thrower remembers a very sudden change in her life at the time of the crash, her life being very much part of her grandparents'. Her dad became a totally different person, she remembers him crying in the middle of the living room with her mum's arm round him. He most likely will have had what is today known as Post Traumatic Stress Disorder (PTSD). He knows now that he wasn't behaving correctly and that it had affected him in a big way. Claire's brother Rob is still traumatised today over the events of 1975.

Stuart was born in Feb 1976 and Lynda regarded him as her present as she had lost Thomas. In the meantime Ken and his brother Peter decided to ride the train from Moorgate to Drayton Park as he felt it was something he had to do as part of the healing process. This small act was one more step towards normality, or as normal as it could be.

Ken used to go round to his mother's for breakfast and one day, three years after the Moorgate crash, he knocked on door as he had forgotten his keys. She shouted to him, "Ken…I've had a stroke," and he immediately smashed the window to gain access. Frances was rushed to hospital where she died four days later. She had never got over the death of her Thomas and she was laid to rest with him at Trent Park.

*

For the survivors of the Moorgate crash they had to rebuild their lives knowing that they were one of the lucky ones. Douglas Thomson had returned to the tube the following Monday, finding out weeks later that Jeff had died in hospital. He suffered for years from high blood pressure and is still affected by the memories of what he saw that day. Like most people he heard the rumours: some included, the driver was diabetic, and in one case the driver was Indian. Like everybody else, he didn't know what was true. (When I interviewed him I put him right on these and a few other false truths.) He would count himself as "extremely lucky" due to the fact he was originally going to travel in the first carriage. Although he went to neither the inquest nor inquiry, he was interviewed by two police officers at his work a few weeks later.

For Barry Coppock he looks back and sees how different his life could have turned out. Why me? Well, why not me? He has had a good life and he always feels like he wants to give something back to society. He feels like Moorgate was his second chance, it could have been him that died that day in the tunnel but for the choice of where he sat on a six-car train. In 2008 he took part in voluntary work for the Stroke Association after his mother had a stroke, highlighting that this could affect anybody (like Ken Thrower's mother years before). Every anniversary he thinks about that day and the people who were not so lucky.

*

Marian King was due to go to Canada, booked with travel agent Thomas Cook, in about the June/July time. Following the injuries sustained in the crash, she had to cancel, but thankfully Thomas Cook gave her a full refund no questions asked after she had explained her circumstances. Marian's mother's parents were from Ireland and at the time they had seen the disaster unfold on the Irish news and rang Marian's mum to ask if their two nieces had been anywhere near as they lived in London and they wanted to make sure they were OK. She then told her that no, her daughter Marian had been in the crash though; by this point the news had gone worldwide. The whole family from Ireland sent her cards as did the children from St Joan of Arc's school who sent some homemade ones to her saying "Get Well Soon", together with some flowers.

Although friends came to see her she never remembered them staying long, although it turns out they did stay a while but she kept drifting in and out of consciousness. A woman in hospital had survived the crash and had lost a lot of blood due to a pole going straight through her leg. She didn't regain consciousness for a whole day, but her daughter Dawn Beard would come and see her. Marian's fiancé Chris had known Dawn for years and he would talk to her in the ward, knowing that she only lived down the road and they had gone to the same school together. Later on they would all go out for a meal on the riverside and discuss old school days and what had united them in the hospital that day.

One day somebody phoned her in the hospital and she took the call. "He said he liked the look of me," she recalls today, and he sent her some flowers. She found this odd and she alerted the staff at the hospital. The flowers turned up with a flowery horseshoe in the middle. She thought this was very strange and told them that if he turned up looking for her she didn't want to meet him. She never found out who it was, he was probably OK and completely innocent, but it freaked her out a little given the circumstances. She told them that she didn't want another call like that. She has, however, kept the horseshoe to this day.

Today she is very jumpy in the presence of sudden loud noises like lorries going past and random bangs. Her stay in hospital was only for two weeks, with a further seven weeks of having her leg in plaster, having to also attend a lot of physiotherapy afterwards to get her muscles working again. As part of her treatment she had to be able to pick up bean bags with her toes, while her mum had to help dress her. "It felt like I was going back to childhood…my leg was very straight and itchy!"

When she eventually returned to work she had a lot of memory trouble, she would take a message on a phone call and immediately forget everything that was said. It took around seven years for her to really feel like she was back to normal. Despite the anxiousness over sudden noise, she never suffered from flashbacks or nightmares which is a blessing considering what she had seen. She would want to talk about it all but would burst into tears, suffering PTSD for a long time. Even before the plaster was taken off her leg she made herself travel back on the tube, finding it very upsetting going back down the steps to the Highbury & Islington platform on the Victoria Line, but despite her mind telling her otherwise, she got back on the train and made the journey.

She started reading a self help book a long time afterwards, after somebody told her she had PTSD. She wanted to find out more information about it; she later realised that there were around twelve elements to it, and it said that "you may usually suffer from 2-3 of these" but she found that she had in fact suffered from all of them! Her family and loved ones helped her a great deal, but after a while the people involved in the crash were no longer helping each other out. "People would say hello to you but it got to a stage where the only thing you had in common was something that you wanted to forget about." Some people recovered in different ways and many ended up not talking about it at all. She had visits from people who would come into the off-licence and see her, they would know her but she didn't seem to know them. It was like everybody had heard of her all of a sudden.

As for her possessions on the train her leather handbag would be returned to her wet and covered in blood, it looked like it had been hosed down at some point but it was not for keeping now. Inside was her little diary with a green/yellow cover, covered in water and blood. She would not get these back till the end of the year and it may have been the personal details on the diary that helped it to be traced back to her.

There was a positive side to the effects of the crash though. Her relationship with Chris Robertson had gone uphill fantastically and over the weeks and months the crash and aftermath had brought them closer together. They realised what would have happened if she had been lost that day and even when she was in hospital he would always stay longer after the family had left for the day. The more he came to see her the more she wanted him around, there was definitely more to their relationship than just being girlfriend and boyfriend. Marian King became Mrs Marian Robertson on 9th October 1981, being married on a Friday as Arsenal were playing the day after and, although they were fans, the disruption would be immense nearby and it was stress that they could be doing without.

As regards compensation she always felt like she was getting to a barrier every time she pursued that avenue. Odd events caused her suspicion of her solicitor and the courts…were they telling her everything or was she being kept in the dark? Eventually she got £2,500 compensation which she spent on a car and going on holiday to help her get over what had happened. At the time of the crash she was learning to drive so this car gave her back some independence that the crash had almost taken away. After thirty-one years at the Nat West bank she left her job and today has a happily married life with Chris at her London home. Her injuries from the crash are evident, she still has numbness in her foot, having to get into the bath with the left foot first so she can make sure the temperature is OK. When she goes to the gym she has to exercise it a lot and keep on top of the physical fitness side of it, keeping the muscles in good working order. To say how badly she was trapped, in the long run her physical injuries were fairly light once the treatment had been effected.

*

Fireman Norman Paulding retired in 1988 before teaming up with the Metropolitan Police as a fire investigating officer. He would go on to work with the police launches and did a lot of training with them until he retired in 1994. Tim Hatton didn't go back to Moorgate for over twenty years. He took part in no police investigation, didn't have a statement taken and did not go to the inquest. A few months later a big reception at the mayor's office at Mansion House was held for the emergency services involved, which the fire crews attended with their colleagues and even took the pump up there to show off. The mayor was chatting to those people who had been involved with the disaster and extended his thanks to all those who had worked hard to bring the survivors out and the bodies of the deceased back to their families. The emergency services couldn't be thanked enough for the incredible jobs they did in the hours and days after the crash in appalling conditions.

A few months later Tim left LFB and was transferred to Bedfordshire till about 1998. He was involved in other incidents through the years, various crashes on the M1 in the 1970s and a petrol tanker explosion in Westoning which made headlines. At 0710 on the morning of 11th September 1976 a Texaco petrol tanker flipped over and slid down the village high street catching fire. The vehicle then exploded. "It looked like an H-bomb had gone off," said Tim as he remembers attending the scene. Homes were destroyed and the fire brigade was there all day, but incredibly there were no fatalities, the only injuries coming from a fire truck that had overturned at the scene.

*

The police officers involved, like the fire service, leave the scene of any disaster to prepare for the next one. The emergency services see death and tragedy on a weekly, in some cases daily, basis and are prepared for the tasks ahead, but in some cases they do not prepare for what stays with them once the job is done. Those involved in Moorgate would all express how much they think about what happened and how the images from inside that train will stay with them forever.

Adrian Eatwell was involved in the investigation into the death of "God's Banker" Roberto Calvi (a man involved in the running of the

Vatican bank who was found hanging from Blackfriars Bridge in 1982 in a case that today is still shrouded in mystery), later on becoming a Detective Constable in CID.

Bud Fisher enjoyed his job with the exception of the final few years, eventually leaving the service in 1980. He was called to neither the inquiry nor the inquest, instead he attended a display of helicopter rescue techniques during a war in Lebanon during the inquest period. His work was continuing into new scenarios and in this case, how people worked at rescues after terrorism, due to the fact that the IRA were very much active at this time. Before and after Moorgate he was involved in other inquiries because of his expertise – the Staines air disaster of 1972, Old Bailey bombing 1973, Tower of London bombing 1974 and Zagreb air disaster 1976. He would notice the difference in police officers over the years; back in the 70s they would be mostly ex servicemen – a very disciplined lot who would use their background of military knowledge to the advantage of the force. He did notice that the lads who were ex pioneer corps had sorted cables and toilets out at Moorgate for ease of the rest of the forces working. After all Fisher's hard work and disaster planning, it is obvious that his work was invaluable that day, saving many lives and getting people seen by doctors faster than normal. For this he would later be awarded the MBE.

Andy Day had been in photographic and forensics since 1969 when he had attended the Moorgate crash. He took hundreds of photographs for the investigation, mostly under the direction of the engineers. Each photo was closely examined by investigators, the coroner and engineers. Day retired in 1993 and became crime scene examiner and crime scene manager with the City of London Police as a civilian. He retired from that job in 2002 then he worked as a senior lecturer at London's Southbank University teaching forensic science until 2007. He loved his police career and by coincidence his son joined the City of London force two weeks after he retired and was awarded collar number 541, his father's old number which he had proudly displayed for thirty-one years. His son would wear the same number for a decade before moving to Chester Constabulary. This bit of news was picked up by the force magazine with the headline: *"As one Day finishes, another begins"*.

Gary Thomas would also be involved in many major incidents over the years. The Old Bailey bombing 1973, *Marchioness* river boat sinking 1989, Canon Street Rail crash 1991 (attending the day after the initial crash) and the Bishopsgate bombing 1992. There were countless other smaller incidents and bombings over the years and he retired from the City of London Police on 30th October 2001, joining the British Transport Police in 2002 where he soon after attended the Potters Bar rail crash.

Tony Wallis recovered the destination board from the front of the train at Moorgate and gave it to the Wood Street Police Museum where it sat behind a glass display for decades with no recognition given to Tony and the work he did that day. (In the making of this book I contacted the City of London police station at Wood Street who placed a small notice on the destination board giving credit for the artefact to Tony.) In the years after he went back to the platform only once as he had to get a train. He found it very strange going back there, later having nightmares about bodies falling onto him. He felt he didn't need counselling as officers at the time just got on with it and moved on, but other than this one period of nightmares the job never really affected him.

As Brian Tibbenham would tell me they didn't have any kind of counselling for those affected and PTSD was not very well recognised back in those days. Mental trauma didn't even come into the equation. "In those days you just spoke to your chief superintendent and he would sit and have a chat with you if something was bothering you." He retired in 1978. Not long after being interviewed for this book, he died in 2011.

Professor Keith Simpson would later go on to examine the body of God's Banker Roberto Calvi in the investigation into his death. He died the day after his seventy-eighth birthday on 21st July 1985.

Daily Telegraph reporter Gerard Kemp, who was the first journalist down in the tunnel to witness the crash, died on 6th January 2009.

London Transport worker Dave Bolton retired early at the age of fifty-seven in 1994. He would be interviewed for the BBC Essex radio programme *In Our Time – A Moorgate Special*. The crew came all the way from Bristol to his house in 2008 and it was broadcast on Radio 4 not long after. In his years working on the London Underground network he remembers the pranks he would play on Ray Deadman. Ray used to report Dave for putting grease on the phone handle and boot polish on the earpiece, so when he would answer the phone he would get a black ear! "He had no sense of humour, he would often say 'it's not dead...man...it's deeeeeed man!' when referring to his name."

Guard Robert Harris disappeared into the realms of history. The company sacked him not long after the crash for his bad timekeeping and he was fined in the April of 1975 for stealing vegetables from a road stall with several others, already having been previously convicted of possessing cannabis.

For WPC Margaret Liles her life did not grind to a halt just because she had lost her foot. Before the crash she had been very athletic and had competed in the No. 9 Police District cross-country championships. The finals were held at Wimbledon Common just months after she had survived the crash. She attended to watch using crutches and although she didn't compete that day, she had previously accumulated enough points to come third overall. She continued working for the police for another year before she was retired on disability pension. The press reported that she was offered a job as civilian staff which would have given her a wage of £2,200 a year. As a policewoman she would have been on only £1,800, giving her a rise!

Ambulanceman Dave Tovey was posted to Wiltshire Ambulance service in 1981 and retired in 2000.

*

Tozammel Syed still tends the grave of his wife Shameen to this day. She is now buried close to her parents who have since passed on. He dreams of her floating in the river today just like the dream her mother had on the day of the crash. He remarried in 1977 and later had two children. He is still married today and lives in Leytonstone, East London.

Javier Gonzalez received a plastic bag while he was still in St Bart's Hospital just days after the crash. This contained his clothes – shrunken after being wet with sweat, dirty and covered in soot. Although all his belongings were recovered, his life as he once knew it would always be still in the tunnel at Moorgate. Looking at the blood stains on the clothes, he realised that it wasn't his blood and it must have come from one of those who had died next to him. This left him feeling like he was in a constant void, unable to fill it knowing so many had died around him.

When police came to his bedside soon after the crash he gave them some names of friends in Scotland who could be informed that he had been in the crash. When the police rang them they automatically assumed that he had been arrested in London for something! As the truth dawned on them they rang Javier's brother who was living in South America to give him the news, who passed it on to his mother. This came as a huge relief because she had seen the news reports and automatically thought her son had died there. It didn't help that he had lied originally saying for her not to worry...he had already spoken to him and he had not been on the train. When the truth emerged and he got the first call he then had to break it to her that Javier was in hospital; needless to say she didn't believe him at first!

As the ambulance had taken him to the hospital he had slipped in and out of consciousness, he was told to relax and try to sleep, but his reply in his semi-conscious state was that he wanted to stay awake as he had never been in an ambulance. Upon arrival they examined him and removed chunks of broken glass from his hair. It was found that he had a broken hip, fracture of the sternum and head injuries. It was most likely these injuries to his head that caused him to have his heaven and hell visions while trapped in the darkness. Due to his head injury he now had to endure a local anaesthetic while the doctors operated on his hip. A nurse held his hand while the procedures took place; he remembers virtually crushing it in the meantime!

He woke up on the Saturday morning to be shown the front page of the newspaper and his name on it. Not being altogether sound of mind at this time, he was instantly shocked...what had he done? Why would he be on the front page...had he robbed a bank or something? When asked if he was on the train he couldn't recall a thing. "What train?" he said, thinking in his head a flash intercity surface train. It took a long time for the truth of what had happened to him the previous day to dawn on him. The word "Moorgate" flashed into his head from looking at the paper, that got him thinking and slowly he remembered the rescue operation and the hospital.

Over the coming days he would receive phone calls and cards from people whom he had never met before in his life. The Salvation Army offered to help along with other religious organisations and police, all realising that a foreign visitor was injured in London and wanting to make sure he was OK. Thankfully he was eventually visited by his brother and he was able to personally ring his mother up to reassure her that he was OK and that he still had use of his legs. It would still be several days before he could move his toes but when that came he was overjoyed.

Javier would spend around two months in hospital in total, but would have to move into a flat that was more easily accessible and walk with crutches for six months until he got his legs back to full working order. It took a long time after this for him to get back on a train when he was well enough again. The tube train would speed into the station and he would simply stand there unable to move while everybody got on and off. Today though, he still lives in London but will forever remember the experiences he had, trapped for five hours in the wreckage of train 272. Whatever it was that happened to him he realises that his life has been handed back to him and he has been given a second chance. There is no way he is going to waste it.

*

Prior to the Moorgate disaster all staff were taught at the White City training centre that the overlap of a signal – that is the distance a train could travel after hitting (being front tripped) at a trainstop (a mechanical device which is raised when a signal is showing red) – was "a SAFE braking distance" i.e. if your train got tripped at a signal you could not come into collision with a train ahead. Following the disaster the word "SAFE" was removed from training courses and an information campaign was launched to attempt to expunge the previous course information. The new training referred merely to "a braking distance".

The accident led to the introduction of TETS, or Trains Entering Terminal Stations (London Underground) or alternatively Moorgate Control (National Rail), named after the disaster and introduced on all dead-end terminal stations. Moorgate control consists of a pair of standard train stop units as used to halt trains that pass red signals. One is installed at the entry to the station platform and one around halfway along the platform. The train stops are normally in the raised position. As the train approaches it moves onto a section of track that initiates a time delay. At the conclusion of the delay, the train stop is lowered allowing the train to pass. The time delay is such that if the train is travelling at more than 10mph its tripcock will hit the train stop before it lowers. This exhausts the air from the braking system applying the emergency brakes. Both train stops have to be lowered to allow the train to leave the station. Like with any disaster, the technology exists but it is always being wise after the event that leads to it being installed.

10. Remembering

After the success of my campaign to have the 1986 Lockington rail disaster recognised, for which I put up a memorial and wrote a book on the disaster, I was contacted by Claire Thrower who had lost her grandfather Thomas in Moorgate. She asked me if I could do the same for them as I had done with the Lockington families. I agreed, but at the same time said that it would take me a while. With forty-three people killed in the middle of London, just those facts alone meant that any memorial would be expensive and time-consuming, as well as the quest to track down people involved after such a long period of time. I began my research into what happened, starting with the obvious – newspapers from the day, blogs on the internet, putting word out in the local Islington newspapers for people to get in touch. Incredibly after over thirty years people were still wanting to talk about it and willing to meet me to discuss their story. I decided to begin raising the money straightaway and got in touch with London Underground for permission to place a plaque up at the station. Their reply was a definite no. "If we put one up for Moorgate then we would have to put one up for everybody who had died on the Underground," was their reasoning. I wrote back explaining that Moorgate wasn't just any death...it was forty-three of them in one of the worst train disasters in Britain. They had already got a plaque each for the three July 7th 2005 Underground bombings, three for the Kings Cross fire of 1987, several others for wartime tragedies (Bethnal Green, Balham). They didn't even reply to this.

So I just did what I did at Lockington – if all else fails then simply find somewhere alternative to place a memorial. Luckily, just a few hundreds yards from the station is Finsbury Square, a few feet from the City of London borders, in the borough of Islington. I got in touch with Islington Council and within three weeks I had permission to put up the memorial. Now it was time to start fundraising!

It took three years of collecting cheques from people – mostly relatives and friends of those who were killed – to get just £1,500 of the £6,000 needed. I could see this was going to be difficult, until I was told of three councillors who worked nearby who would be willing to help. They agreed to fund the remaining £4,500 completely, and with the money handed over on 16th July 2012 in a "big cheque" ceremony for the papers it was time to have the monument made. I had already designed the wording, taking the names from the coroner's office who sent me a letter listing them all. Unfortunately there were some major spelling errors many of which I did correct myself through research, but even today there are several names that are slightly wrong.

Then along came the protesters. As part of anti-capitalist protests around the UK, people started camping out at St Paul's Cathedral for several months, living in tents and vandalising the general area until the police had them moved on. The only downside to their being evicted was that they decided Finsbury Square would be their next home. In just a few weeks the entire square was like a muddy battlefield, strewn with litter and camp fires. Thankfully Islington Council once again came to the rescue after they had all been once again relocated. The entire area was re-turfed and metal fencing was placed around where the memorial was going to be. It had gone from having a simple monument to having a memorial garden! This was even better than expected.

With the memorial not ready for the next anniversary in February 2013 the earliest we could have any kind of dedication ceremony was later on in the summer, so I organised 28th July for that ceremony to take place. Thanks go to James Bowyer (the work colleague of Antony Byczkowski) who put me in touch with the Lord Lieutenant of London and the Archdeacon of St Paul's who agreed to attend and speak at the ceremony. With the word being spread over the internet it was now a waiting game to see how many people would turn up.

*

On the morning of the ceremony I had already been in London for three days to consolidate a lot of my research and to interview new people involved in the disaster. It was an exciting time for many of the relatives as this was what had been missing from the story all along; at last now there was going to be recognition that this was no longer a forgotten disaster despite it being the seventh worst rail crash in the United Kingdom.

As I made my way to Finsbury Square the sun was beating down to the point where jackets were hung on the backs of chairs and sunglasses were out, a beautiful day with the heat rising by the hour. I had scheduled the ceremony to take place at 11am, so turning up nice and early would ensure the memorial was covered up and the area set up in good time. As expected there were a lot of people who were coming up to me asking about it: Who was I? What was my connection? Did I lose anybody in the crash? There were some old faces that I had already seen previously – the Wonderlings, Throwers, Halls and Newsons – and there were some that I had never seen before – the Mayalekes, Shahs, Marks – who all wanted to talk about their loss and tell me more about their story. I could have stayed there all day and not heard everything I wanted to hear so instead I took email addresses and contact numbers and told them I would arrange to meet with them at a later date. One of them was the wife of Jeff Benton who was now living in South Africa and had literally just flown in the previous night to attend the ceremony. By now crowds were starting to form as the ceremony itself was being finalised between ourselves. A guard of honour made up of police officers and firefighters in full uniform were at the back, joining the emergency services that had been in the tunnel on that dreadful week back in 1975: FANY and Salvation Army representatives, London Ambulance Service, WRVS, London Underground and various other interested people who wanted to pay their respects.

I started by introducing myself and giving the crowd a brief outline of why we were here today before turning over to Claire Thrower. She told how her entire family's lives had been turned upside down on that day, how they had hoped for a memorial for over thirty-eight years and how the years had gone by with nothing. A lot of people in the audience could definitely relate to her words and all shared the same outlook and thoughts. Next came the Lord Lieutenant who gave a very dignified speech before slowly pulling the cloth off the monument with the Archdeacon. Cameras flashed, film rolled as the moment they had all waited for was finally here. A blessing took place over the silent crowd before I stood once again to read the names of those inscribed on the memorial and hold a minute's silence. I thought it appropriate to show the world just how much gratitude the families had towards those who had been there back in 1975, so factored in a public display of thanks to all those rescuers, volunteers, investigators and even those who gave blood from the streets. Rounds of applause were heard around the square as the men who worked in the tunnel stood in dignified silence, proud of their work, proud of being part of a team that saved lives. Tributes were then laid at the base of the memorial one by one as cameras once again captured the raw grief that was still as strong today as it had been then. Marian Robertson said this was the first time she had ever seen any of the families together since the crash.

After the ceremony it was down the road to The Globe Inn just a few yards away from Moorgate station. I had organised a buffet, very kindly paid for by the Throwers, and this gave people a chance to meet each other for the first time in years and properly converse. Families with such a strong connection who could relate to each other's suffering and heartache. A group of London Underground drivers, one of whom had just come off a nightshift and had not even been to bed, talked about how Les Newson was "one of their own" and they had come to remember him most of all. Like brothers in arms, the London Underground is more than just a bunch of executives and whizz kids that the papers focus on, it is a family.

Unfortunately due to the major newspapers like the Evening Standard not taking an interest in the memorial, a lot of the families only heard about it on the news that night. I was contacted by several people asking me why I had not informed them and it was simply this – the papers hadn't written about it (apart from the Islington Gazette/Tribune), I didn't have any contact details from 1975 and there was no way I was to know these people even existed. Needless to say research can only go so far, but I was happy that they had got in touch and I could tell them of the work so far and they all agreed to tell their stories for this book.

*

It was in late 2013 that I was contacted by Tom Motyka from Albavideo who said he wanted to make a documentary about the disaster. I put him in touch with several people who would be willing to make a contribution to his film and the finished result saw interviews with Tim Hatton (fireman) George Mackmurdie (son of George), Ken Thrower and myself. I felt it was the right time to make public my findings into the research I had done. The filming commenced in January 2014 and Tom got to work on introducing it to the relevant film companies for it to appear on national television. At the time of writing the film has not yet been released.

Soon after the opening of the memorial it was announced by London Underground that they too would be putting up a plaque, this would be done on the next anniversary at the station itself. Now at first I was very angry…the whole reason I spent three years of my life on the memorial was because they had refused to have anything to do with it. Now they were saying yes to a plaque without a problem. Laurence Marks was quoted in the newspapers as saying that they were "shamed" into putting it up because they had done nothing for almost four decades and had found it all a bit embarrassing. However, it was down to Tony Hall from London Underground; that was the reason for the decision. For Tony had a very special reason for wanting it...his sister Terry was one of the victims.

With exactly seven months to the day to organise, London Underground contacted me to help spread the word of their plaque to the families and survivors, which I agreed to do. By now I had come round to the fact that they had at last chose to recognise that Moorgate was not just a disaster, it was a disaster in their name. I had spoken to their teams several times who told me what the plan was and for the plaque not to be a rival of the Finsbury Square memorial, but rather to complement it. It would contain no names but it would be a metre high on the outside of the station wall so people could see it and view it without having to pay to get through ticket barriers and go down into the station itself.

On Friday 28th February 2014 I took an early train to London to meet up with the drivers who I had now come to know as personal friends of mine. We discussed the crash and the conspiracies over coffee and breakfast before heading off to pay our respects at the memorial which was done almost to the minute of the crash thirty-nine years earlier. Gathering at the side of Moorgate station I was once again shaking hands with friends that I had made over the last few years. As the ceremony started at 11am, Lord Mayor Fiona Wolff CBE paid tribute to all those involved in rescuing the survivors at Moorgate before pulling the curtains open to reveal the plaque. The Archdeacon was once again called in to give a blessing and then tributes were laid at the base. The entire ceremony was just ten minutes long, but staying around afterwards got me in touch with several new people who I chatted to for hours after. The family of Tony Byczkowski wanted to tell me all about their genius boy who had had his life cut short so suddenly. Geoff Marsh's sister had flown all the way from New Zealand and made a lot of new contacts to keep in touch with. And firefighter Brian Goodfellow was introduced to the woman he rescued – Eileen Fleming (née Smith). With tears in their eyes they recounted how Brian had dragged her upwards out of the wreckage and led her to safety. For them it was a huge relief and a bit of closure, to see that nearly four decades later she was alive and kicking in front of him.

Javier Gonzalez wrote a book which was published at the start of 2015 detailing how the crash affected his life and telling his story in depth, of the hours spent trapped in the wreckage and how he had a vision of heaven and hell before being rescued. At the time of writing a BBC documentary series is being put together to reunite survivors of disasters with their rescuers, one episode will focus on Moorgate and again I put them in touch with some of my contacts. Again Brian Goodfellow would meet a woman whom he helped in the wreckage – that of Marian Robertson.

So after the years of research my Moorgate project is over with some very good results. I would like to think that people have taken comfort in talking to me and having their stories heard finally. I hope that the ridiculous conspiracies are laid to rest and that the driver Les Newson can finally be recognised for the hero that he was, both in wartime and at his work. I am pleased that there are now two memorials to commemorate what happened at Moorgate and that people will be going to pay their respects there for many years to come. Writing this book is part of that memorial, showing the world that heroes do not wear capes and leap from buildings, they wear overalls and breathing apparatus, facemasks and uniforms. They carry bags of tools and cameras, IV drips and stretchers.

But like the fictional superheroes, these too disappear into the night, waiting for the next job of saving lives.

Laurence Marks

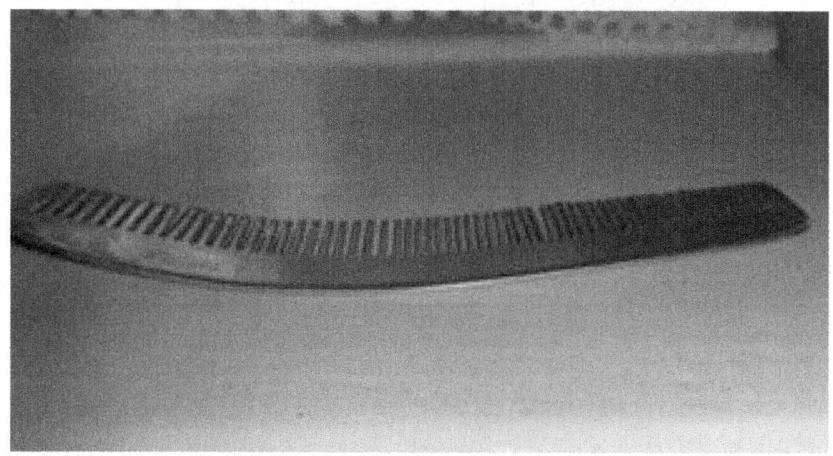

Comb found on body of Antony Byczkowski showing the damage inflicted in the crash

Card from the wreath sent by Arsenal FC to the funeral of Thomas Thrower

Plaque on the door of the Benton rescue room

For Steve

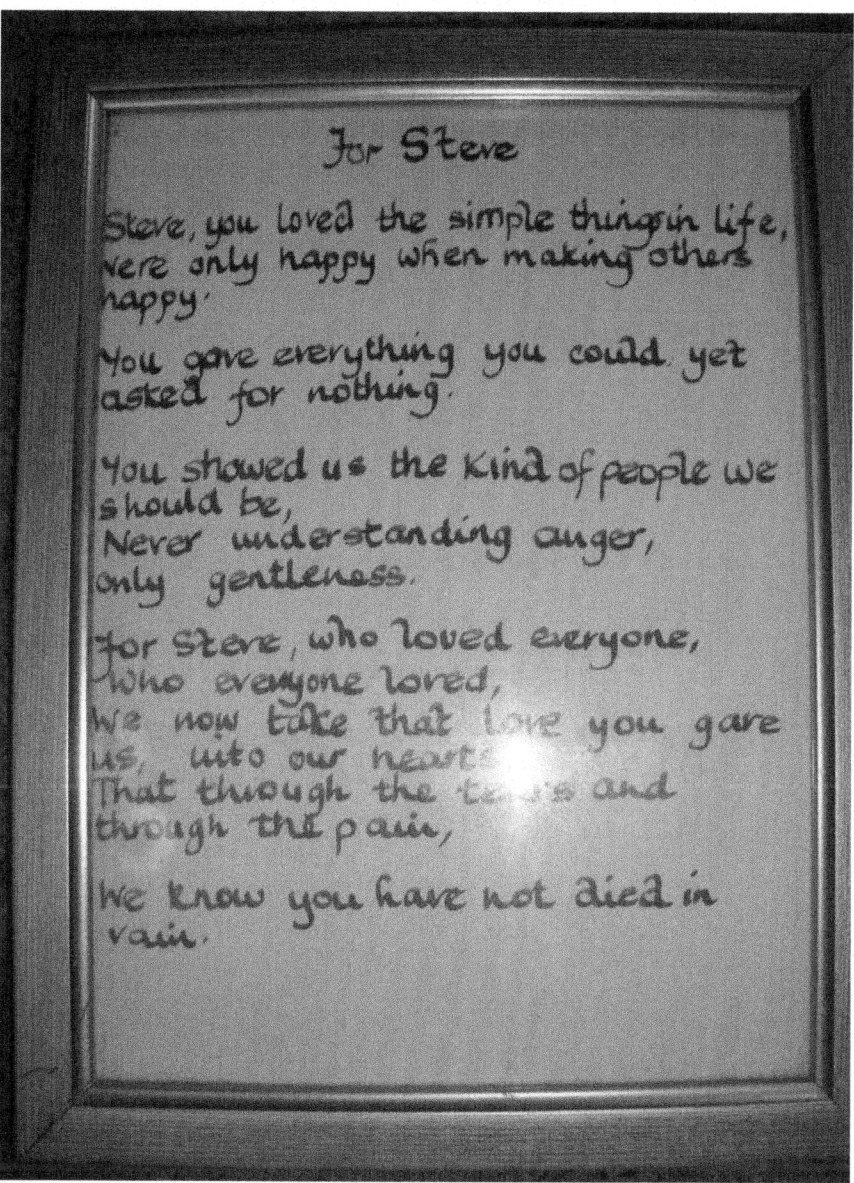

Steve, you loved the simple things in life,
Were only happy when making others happy.

You gave everything you could, yet asked for nothing.

You showed us the kind of people we should be,
Never understanding anger,
Only gentleness.

For Steve, who loved everyone,
Who everyone loved,
We now take that love you gave us, into our hearts
That through the tears and through the pain,

We know you have not died in vain.

Poem to Stephen Payne

Jeff Benton funeral flowers

Moorgate destination board which today is on display at
Wood Street Police Station Museum

Grave of Elizabeth Marsden, Islington Cemetery

Grave of Fred Wonderling, Camden Cemetery

George Mackmurdie's grave

Galaeera Lombardo's grave,
Islington Cemetery

Grave of Janice Donovan

Grave of Galaeera Lombardo, Islington Cemetery

Grave of Joan Phelps, Islington Cemetery

Shameen Syed's grave, Bangladesh

Terry Hall's grave, Manor Park Cemetery - 25th May 2014

Grave of Kathleen Hughes, Islington Cemetery

Grave of Rosemarie Mansi, Islington Cemetery

Thomas Thrower's grave

Helen Newson with grandson Robert during BBC interview - circa 1976

Annette Byczkowska at her Brighton home in 2014 holds the doll her brother Antony Byczkowski bought her in the 1970s

Survivor Javier Gonzalez (November 2013)

Moorgate thimble commemorating the 25th anniversary

Memorial opening - 28th July 2013

Marian King four months after the crash at her 21st birthday

Marian 38 years later at the memorial unveiling

London Underground plaque unveiling - 28th February 2014

The family of Antony Byczkowski plant an olive tree at the memorial on the 40th anniversary of the crash

Afterword

The 40th anniversary of the Moorgate disaster has just passed, the grief, which shows no sign of abating, still very much apparent in a lot of people. While there was no official remembrance ceremony, each family and individual had their own way of remembering the day their lives changed forever. Some survivors stayed with their families, some laid flowers at the Finsbury Square monument, others simply had a quiet day of reflection. The Byczkowska family had permission from Islington Council to place an olive tree next to the memorial and this they did on 28th February 2015.

It was at this point, as this book was going to print, that I was contacted by Cathy Higgins whose sister was 19-year-old Rosemarie Mansi who had died in the crash. With just days to go until being printed I arranged an interview and was able to tell her story and include it here today.

On the morning of the crash Rosie had been staying with a friend and their family and would have left from Bounds Green heading into the City, as she was a student at the City of London Polytechnic doing languages and secretarial studies. Her dream was to work at the United Nations office in Brussels and she had deliberately chosen a shorter course so she would start this career at the earliest opportunity. Living with her brother Tom and their mother over in Wood Green, she was a very vibrant young woman who always liked to get stuck into things, becoming a Queens Guide and being heavily involved in local church activities. Rosie was clearly an intelligent woman academically and was always known by her family as being "full of life".

As the news filtered out into the wider world of a major incident at Moorgate, 22-year-old Cathy was sat on a train herself heading into London from Maidenhead, final destination Hammersmith, to attend a celebration. Hearing what was going on she contacted her brother and mother who had said that they had not heard from her but that it was nothing to worry about. It was most likely absolute chaos with people everywhere and the best thing to do was wait to see when she rang home. This never happened, and as she was leaving the party the family became worried when nobody had seen Rosie all day. They decided to ring the emergency line and hospitals. Neither had a Rosemarie Mansi on their lists, but they kept ringing for several days, with the same results. They began to wonder where she was… did she even get on the train that day? The waiting was agony, all kinds of stories going round in their heads, hoping that she would turn up wondering what all the fuss was about.

But their worst fears were realised when, on 4th March, a call from the coroner asked them to come and identify a body. Although Dr Paul was very sympathetic and helpful to them, it did not extinguish the sudden realisation that the items before them at his office were Rosie's: her camel-haired coat, handbag, an earring and her ID card with photograph. They asked to see her body, to which he very tactfully told them that it would not be possible. In their state of mind they never thought for a minute what four days in a tunnel would do to her. Looking back at that conversation today Cathy realises why. But today was doubly poignant for the family – it was twelve years to the day since their father had died at the age of fifty-two.

In the days after the disaster they found London Underground very unhelpful. Although they never claimed compensation (their mother was a very proud woman and would not have asked anybody for anything) they were asked to fill in a form for any expenses they had incurred. When they put down the cost of travel to the airport and a wreath, it was questioned by the very people who had told them to do it. Finding their entire attitude disgusting, they have never forgotten they way they were treated.

The memories of Rosie have not diminished with time. She was Cathy's bridesmaid at her wedding in 1974 and both Cathy and her brother Tom will always remember the pretty young woman with high cheekbones and dark hair who had so much to live for. Their mother lived until she was ninety-two years old after raising three children on her own and having a very hard time with paralysis for several years after Cathy was born.

Rosie was buried in Islington Cemetery with her father where she remains today amongst several other victims of the Moorgate crash. Looking around the quiet roads in this huge mass of graves there are familiar names – Fred Wonderling, Joan Phelps, Elizabeth Marsden, Lina Vella Lombardo and Kathleen Hughes. Many more were cremated here and their ashes scattered.

As the years go by many more people will want to talk about their experiences at Moorgate, I wish I could put everybody's story in the book so it is preserved forever, alas that would not be possible. I have included as many as possible after four and a half years of tracking people down. Most people I spoke to were very welcoming and happy to have their sons, daughters, husbands and wives remembered. I wrote this book for these people and others like them to share their stories, and for this to be another memorial to that day in 1975 when disaster came to the London Underground.

For me I have found this a very unique journey, I have met some brave and very dignified people, some of whom I class as personal friends today. As you read this book and take in the stories of the normal everyday people who were brought together by this one event, I am already researching another forgotten disaster. A stone memorial and a plaque is never enough to remember these events, it must also be told in print to give those names etched in stone a true face and a story that will live forever in words and pictures. Only then do you know who those people are.

Richard Jones
March 2015

Appendix A - Disasters and accidents on the London Underground

Date	Casualties	Details
2 January 1885	0 casualties	Bomb at Gower Street (now Euston Square) on Metropolitan Line train.
26 April 1897	1 killed, 60 injured	Anarchist bombing on Metropolitan Railway train at Aldersgate Station (now Barbican).
5 December 1905	6 killed, 8 injured	Roof collapse at Charing Cross.
26 April 1924	5 killed, 70 injured	Outside Euston Station between tube train and mainline train.
27 August 1928	74 injured	Train hits buffers at Euston Station
10 March 1938	12 injured	Two Northern Line trains collide between Waterloo and Charing Cross.
17 May 1938	6 killed, 43 injured	Train hits back end of stationary carriages of another train while in a tunnel between Charing Cross and Temple on District Line.
3 February 1939	2 injured	IRA bombs exploded in left luggage offices at Tottenham Court Road and Leicester Square stations.
3 March 1943	173 Killed, 100+ injured	A stampede of people at the entrance to Bethnal Green station during what was believed to be an air raid, but turned out to be British guns being tested making people panic into thinking they were being bombed.
31 December 1945	3 killed	Two Metropolitan Line trains collide in fog in open air section near Northwood.
27 July 1946	1 killed	Driver suffers heart attack and dead man's handle fails causing train to hit buffers at Edgware on Northern Line.

08 April 1953	12 killed	Two trains collide in single track tunnel between Stratford and Leyton on the Central Line.
28 July 1958	1 killed	Fire on train on Central Line at Holland Park.
11 August 1960	Several injuries	Fire on train at Redbridge. Passengers and crew suffer smoke inhalation and are evacuated.
26 December 1973	0 injuries	IRA bomb explodes in phone booth at Sloane Square station booking hall.
28 February 1975	43 killed, 76 injured	Train overshoots end tunnel at Moorgate platform 9 and hits brick wall.
15 March 1976	1 killed, 2 injured	IRA bombing premature detonation on Metropolitan Line at West Ham station leaves terrorist shooting one man dead and another injured before shooting himself. Bomber survives.
16 March 1976	1 injured	IRA bombing of empty train injures one person on platform at Wood Green station.
9 July 1980	21 injured	Collision between two westbound trains at Holborn station, Central Line
21 June 1981	1 killed 16 injured	Fire in tunnel at Goodge Street on Northern Line.
11 August 1982	18 injured	Fire in train at Bounds Green, Piccadilly Line.
20 August 1984	1 killed 32 injured	Collision between two trains near Leyton station on Central Line.
23 November 1984	14 injured	Fire in Oxford Circus station resulting in all casualties being due to smoke inhalation.
11 December 1984	1 killed 6 injured	Train ran into back of stationary train at Kilburn on Central Line.
18 November 1987	31 killed	Fire swept through ticket hall at Kings Cross station after escalator fire caused by failure to clean dirt from under it.
23 December 1991	0 injuries	IRA bombs placed on trains at Neasden and Harrow on the Hill detonate.

7 February 1992	0 injuries	IRA bomb detonates at Barking station.
24 April 1999	0 injuries	Derailment soon after leaving Gunnersbury Station. Passengers evacuated safely.
25 January 2003	32 injured	Derailment on Central Line at Chancery Lane.
11 May 2004	21 injured	Derailment on Central Line between Bethnal Green and Mile End.
17 October 2003	0 injuries	Derailment on Piccadilly Line near Hammersmith.
19 October 2003	7 injured	Derailment on Northern Line at Camden Town station.
7 July 2005	52 killed, 750 injured (Includes 13 killed on bus)	Suicide bombers detonate explosives near Kings Cross, Aldgate and Edgware Road, then a fourth bomb is detonated on a bus above ground.
21 July 2005	One killed in shooting following day by mistake	Suicide bombers attempt to repeat attacks of previous two weeks. Bombs fail to detonate and perpetrators go on the run, recaptured after a massive manhunt.
5 July 2007	21 injured	Derailment on Central Line between Bethnal Green and Mile End stations.
13 August 2010	0 injuries	Broken down maintenance locomotive becomes uncoupled and rolls away on its own for several stations before coming to a stop near Warren Street.

Not included in this list is the amount of damage and casualties caused by the bombings of the Second World War 1939-1945. Three of the worst incidents occurred when German bombers scored a direct hit on Balham station (64-68 killed – the death toll has always been debated), Bank station (56 killed) and Bounds Green station (19 killed).

Also not included are any terrorist devices that were defused before they could explode. There have been several of these planted by the IRA which were dealt with at the time. Any that did detonate are included in the table.

Appendix B - List of those killed in or as a result of the Moorgate crash

Benton, Jeffrey David
Boggis, Stanley Ernest Clyde
Bradbury, Peter
Byczkowski, Antony Lucious
Chan, Hian Oon
Cook, Janet Marie
Corking, Albert Frederick
Crotty, Adrian Peter
Donovan, Janice Patricia
Edwards, Kenneth Gareth
Eva, Sidney
Gale, Charles Ronald
Georgiades, Threse Viki
Genin, Cecil Adaine Leonard John
Gordon, Alistair
Halford, Barbara Jessie
Hall, Theresa Helen
Hughes, Gillian Mary
Hobbs, Henry Patrick
Hughes, Kathleen Veronica
Lombardo, Lina Vella
Mackmurdie, George

Maddocks-Watson, Michael John
Mansi, Rosemarie
Marks, Bernard
Marsh, Geoffrey Charles
Marsden, Elizabeth Christine
Mayaleke, Sherifat Adebukonla
Nazim, Alla-Uddin
Nazim, Nazikan
Newson, Leslie Benjamin
O'Brien, Mary Teresa
Payne, Stephen Kenneth
Phelps, Joan
Prevost, Donald Robert
Redfearn, David Peter
Shah, Chiman Mahanlil
Simpson, Jane
Syed, Shameen Banu
Thrower, Thomas Henry
Ward, Colin
Wilson, David
Wonderling, Frederick John

Acknowledgements

Claire and Ken Thrower
George Mackmurdie
Steve O'Brien
Janet Grove
Laurence Marks
Freda, Annette and Margarita Byczkowska
Diane and Vincent Proudfoot
Sandra and Robert Newson
Leslie Cook
Sheila Payne
Marie Therese Crotty
Fred, Carol and Sammy Wonderling
Family of Teresa Hall
Keith Benton
Joan and Fred Donovan
Stella Gordon
Valerie Stockley
Brenda, Carol and Jean Wilson
Cathy Higgins
Barry Coppock
Douglas Simpson
Margaret Liles
Marian Robertson
Eileen Fleming
Javier Gonzalez
John Baldwin
John Palser
Gary Fitzgerald
Amanda Day
Peter Hingle
Dylan Glenister
Paula Reynolds
Helen Robinson
Stephanie Rousseau
David Bolton
David Tovey
Tony Wallis
Gary Thomas
Frances McPherson

Brian Tibbenham
Brian Fisher
Andy Day
Alan Frances
Adrian Eatwell
Bob Barnes
Sylvia and Brian Goodfellow
Frank David
Norman Paulding
Paul Efreme
Bob Ainsworth
Tim Hatton
Patrick Roberts
Petra Laidlaw
Peter Simmons
John Baldwin
James Bowyer
Catherine Coulthard
Allan Grice
Len Harley
Alan Howson
London Fire Brigade
City of London Police
London Metropolitan Archives
Guildhall Library
Islington Gazette - Tristan Barclay
Islington Tribune - Peter Gruner
SUDEP (Sudden Death in Epilepsy)
Epilepsy Action
Islington and Camden Cemeteries
London Transport Museum
ASLEF
British Red Cross
Mirrorpix
Mary Evans Picture Library
Rex Features

For their help with the 2013 memorial

Sir David Brewer - Lord Lt of London
Archdeacon of London The Venerable David Meara
Andy O'Loughlin (London Fire Brigade)
David Rushton - Chaplain Royal London Hospitals
Barry Lucas - Head of Highways, Islington
London Ambulance Service
London Fire Brigade
City of London Police
Transport for London/London Underground staff
Juliette Jones
Sue and Graham Lovegrove
First Aid Nurses Yeomanry
Salvation Army
Royal Voluntary Services
The Globe Inn, Moorgate
Troy Gallagher
Robert Khan
Claudia Webbe
City of London coroner
Crays Hill Memorials
Dave Bamford - Islington Council

Further Reading

Books

1. Moorgate: Anatomy of a rail disaster - Sally Holloway
2. Keeping the Balls in the air - Alan Francis
3. Call the Fire Brigade - Allan Grice
4. A ticket to eternity - Javier Gonzalez

Reports and articles

1. Report on the Accident that occurred on 28th February 1975 at Moorgate Station - Her Majesty's Stationery Office.
2. Readers Digest - February 1976 - Death Ride Under London by Peter Browne.
3. Woman - 4th March 1978 - A Train To Nowhere.
4. Rail magazine – March 2015 (40th anniversary article).

TV appearances

1. Me, My Dad and Moorgate (2006, Channel 4)
2. Real Lives Reunited – Episode 8 (2015, BBC1)
3. The Nationwide Report (1976, BBC)